THE
SACRED
ART

THE
SACRED
ART

GROWING FAITHFUL DISCIPLES IN THE 21st CENTURY

JOHNNY TURNER

TATE PUBLISHING & *Enterprises*

 Tate Publishing
& Enterprises

Tate Publishing is committed to excellence in the publishing industry. Our staff of highly trained professionals, including editors, graphic designers, and marketing personnel, work together to produce the very finest books available. The company reflects the philosophy established by the founders, based on Psalms 68:11,

"The Lord Gave The Word And Great Was The Company Of Those Who Published It."

If you would like further information, please contact us:
1.888.361.9473 | www.tatepublishing.com
Tate Publishing & *Enterprises*, LLC | 127 E. Trade Center Terrace
Mustang, Oklahoma 73064 USA

The Sacred Art: Growing Faithful Disciples in the Twenty-First Century
Copyright © 2007 by Dr. Johnny Turner. All rights reserved.

No part of this publication may be reproduced, stored in a retrieval system or transmitted in any way by any means, electronic, mechanical, photocopy, recording or otherwise without the prior permission of the author except as provided by USA copyright law.

All scripture quotations, unless otherwise noted, are taken from the Holy Bible, New International Version ®, Copyright © 1973, 1978, 1984 by International Bible Society. Used by permission of Zondervan Publishing House. All rights reserved.

The opinions expressed by the author are not necessarily those of Tate Publishing, LLC.

This book is designed to provide accurate and authoritative information with regard to the subject matter covered. This information is given with the understanding that neither the author nor Tate Publishing, LLC is engaged in rendering legal, professional advice. Since the details of your situation are fact dependent, you should additionally seek the services of a competent professional.

Book design copyright © 2007 by Tate Publishing, LLC. All rights reserved.
Cover design by Elizabeth A. Mason
Interior design by Lynly D. Taylor

Published in the United States of America

ISBN: 978-1-5988687-2-2
07.08.06

This book is dedicated to every believer who is passion driven to Growing Faithful Disciples. Those pastors and churches whose hearts have been ignited with love to envision to see the disciple ministry implemented is commendable. The methods and principles in this book are needed for the church to really participate in rediscovering the sacred art of discipleship. The church is here on earth to make a difference in *shaping and growing lives for eternity.* I am grateful to the loving parishioners of the Bethelite Institutional Baptist Church, Brooklyn, New York where I have the opportunity to serve as pastor to complete this project.

It is also dedicated to my wife and supporter in ministry, Patricia Turner and our son, Jonathan who aspires to publish one day. It was their enthusiasm which added to the implementation of these principles for the glory of God.

Acknowledgments

Through the many years, this book would not have been completed without the guidance of the Holy Spirit and the prayers of many faithful friends and other supportive family members. I am deeply indebted to the following individuals:

To my wife, Patricia Turner and supporter in ministry. To senior pastor, Rick Warren of the Saddleback Church, Lake Forest, CA, thank you for encouraging me to pursue writing. Dr. Edward Wheeler, president of the Christian Theological School, Indianapolis, IN, thank you for your suggestions and patience in providing valuable feedback.

Thanks to pastor Jim Cymbala of Brooklyn Tabernacle, Brooklyn, NY, for your inspiring insights, advice and encouragements to take a look at the manuscript. To Dr. Harold Carter, senior pastor of Shiloh Baptist Church, Baltimore, MD, for your willingness to agree to write the foreword. Dr. Allen Paul Weaver, senior pastor of Bethesda Baptist, New Rochelle, NY, thank you for your suggestions, encouragements, and support in the publication of this book.

To the following parishioners where I serve as pastor, Bethelite Institutional Baptist Church, Brooklyn, NY: June Allgood, Roselle Wright, Lonnette Allgood, and Charlane Conner for helping to proof the manuscript in its early stages. Thank you Marilyn Thornton for your encouragement.

Special thanks to Fannie Flono, associate editor at the Charlotte Observer, Charlotte, NC, for critiquing the final proof for publication.

Contents

Foreword 11
Preface 13

Seven Essentials For Understanding Discipleship 15

Introduction: Why Should the Church Care About
    Making Disciples? 19

PART ONE: THE FOUNDATION FACTOR 31
    Chapter 1
      A Sure Foundation:
      Developing a Theology of Discipleship 33
    Chapter 2
      A Strong Foundation:
      Understanding the Biblical Plan of
      Discipleship for God's Church. 49
    Chapter 3
      A Revolutionary Foundation:
      Implementing the Missionary Mandate 77

PART TWO: THE HARVEST FACTOR. 103
    Chapter 4
      Responding to the Harvest:
      What the Church Should Do. 105

Chapter 5
>   The Results of Harvest Work:
>   Growing a Healthy Church 143

Chapter 6
>   True Love for the Harvest:
>   Philippi: Being a Faithful and
>   Loving Church 171

PART THREE: THE POWER FACTOR 199

Chapter 7
>   The Church Utilizing Power through Conflict:
>   Engaging in Spiritual Warfare 201

Chapter 8
>   The Church's Most Respected Identity:
>   Having the Power to Stand 227

Chapter 9
>   The Church's Life–long Purpose:
>   Praying with Power 245

Chapter 10
>   Embracing Social Justice with Power:
>   The Church's Radical Identity 261

Appendix 1
>   The Disciple's Pledge 273

Appendix 2
>   A Theology of Discipleship 275

Epilogue 277
Endnotes 281
Bibliography 289

Foreword

There will never be a "church generation" in which a fresh word about discipleship development is not needed. The heart of the gospel message calls for renewal in Christ as Savior and as Lord, one generation after another. When this work is not effectively done, the life of the total church suffers.

In our present world, true discipleship development is under great attack by a secular culture that seeks to destroy the mandate of the Great Commission. Rather than hearing the Word of our Lord to "make disciples," so much of the church seems to be absorbed in the work of religiously entertaining the flock with pleasing words and non-demanding ministries. The church simply cannot remain true to her call and be effective if the present course of action is maintained.

This book, *The Sacred Art: Growing Faithful Disciples in the Twenty-First Century*, is a clarion call to the Church of God to move beyond the winds of comfort in church life, that are blowing in from the wider society today. The call of this book to renew our faith by growing in the principles of faith laid out by Jesus Christ will build stronger believers and move them into effective ministries in Christ. It is indeed a book for all Christian workers and believers who seek relevance *in* the faith and a deeper commitment *to* the faith, once delivered into the saints.

Dr. Harold A. Carter

Pastor
New Shiloh Baptist Church
Baltimore, Maryland

Preface

The Reverend Johnny Turner is a man on a mission. The mission is to fulfill the gospel mandate to "make disciples." *The Sacred Art* is Turner's attempt to help churches move their members toward the goal of being disciples. Turner believes that unless the church focuses on making disciples, the future effectiveness of the church is in jeopardy. *The Sacred Art* seeks to provide a theological and biblical basis for the work of making disciples. However, the book is clearly focused on a pastor's perspective of what works in a local congregation. The chapter review guides provide important learning benchmarks that help make the book an important teaching tool. The Sacred Art is a practical guide to disciple training that engages the whole church in this important work.

Evangelism has been and remains an important aspect of the church's ministry. *The Sacred Art* expands the conversation beyond how to bring people into the church to how do you help people mature as Christians. That maturity is the key to how effective the ministry of the church will be in the 21st Century.

Edward L. Wheeler, *President*

Christian Theological Seminary
Indianapolis, Indiana

Seven Essentials *for* Understanding Discipleship

After the reading of each chapter, there is a section called "Study Review Guide." This section is designed for you to think about what you have engaged in regarding each study. They are:

Biblical Truth This is the key to understanding what you have learned. The biblical truth is the driving point of what has been learned and you can reflect and apply the truth to your life. Jesus said, "To the Jews who had believed him, Jesus said, "If you hold to my teaching, you are really my disciples. Then you will know the truth, and the truth will set you free" (John 8: 31–32).

Memory Verse There is power in memory. There is influence in memory. When we remember, it inspires people and amazes them on how much we remember. Remembering scripture is a powerful tool and will be a great asset in your walk with Jesus. The verse for each review is a verse to remember to reflect on that chapter.

Key Word The key word is a word that focuses on the overall study for each chapter review. Each key word will have a Greek word to explain the meaning and context for each review. It will help one to reflect biblically and theologically regarding discipleship.

Point of Emphasis When we learn, we need to know what is important for a particular emphasis and context. The object of the point of emphasis is to help us to summarize what we need to reflect on.

Theological Reflection Every believer should have a theological view about God, Jesus, the Holy Spirit and for this study, discipleship. Theological reflection is simply what you know about what you have studied. One must reflect on where he or she stands relative to faith. It is what you can say in the context of theology regarding the significance of discipleship.

Personal Application Your thoughts on the importance of how this study has impacted you. Personal application is how you implement what you have studied. This is your personal testimony of what discipleship is saying to you. To learn and not apply is a waste of time. Make the most out of what you have done. Personal application will enrich your experience as a disciple.

Study Questions It is important to engage in the study questions. The purpose of the questions is to eliminate passivity. You can do it alone or in a group. It is suggested that you get with others and share. More minds are better than one. In fact, we learn from others. It is amazing how someone else can add light to a concept, truth or story when another has something totally different. Sharing thoughts will make a difference and leave a lasting impact on the individual and the group. Studying together can inspire each to engage even when others may be passive. However, it has been known that some in a group will wait for others to give the answer. In order to grow deeper, the questions will be helpful.

Introduction

Why Should The Church Care About Making Disciples?

The purpose of this book is to encourage those who are interested in maximizing the growth of a church by using new insights for growing healthy disciples. These insights address concerns for churches of all faiths or denominations. However, there will be times when I will make reference to the African American church tradition as an example for disciple-making. This is because I am a pastor of an African American church. Historically, many churches do not have a full understanding of what it means to grow healthy disciples. It has been asked over and over, "What is a disciple?" The padded answers have always been: a follower and/or a learner of Jesus Christ. That answer does not really stick; it does not drive home the practicality of the true meaning of discipleship. It is a quick answer and people move on without real answers.

African American churches in the early 1800s until about 1950 were filled with people. They had a passion for revivals.

Adequate preparation went into the planning of the revival. There were two weeks, one for praying and one for preaching. This was a positive aspect of discipleship. This was different from any other church tradition in America. During this time people were close and shared in nurturing new converts. This was part of the discipleship process and plan.

"What does it mean to follow Jesus?" is a fair question. It means to be totally committed, loyal and faithful. It really is taking risks and walking strong when criticized. Many think that just coming to church is discipleship, or even in some circles, churches with large attendance. In chapter two, I will share deeper insights on what it means to be a disciple.

The central thesis of this book is that churches *grow disciples and keep them nurtured and healthy for ministry.* My argument is that many churches have a deficit in the area of discipleship. Churches will mushroom when they utilize proven methods and approaches within mainline denominations regarding rediscovering the sacred art of discipleship. This means that another church should share discipleship principles and methods with other churches.

As pastor of the Bethelite Institutional Baptist Church, Brooklyn, New York, I am in the process of growing healthy disciples for the glory of God. Here is what we are doing. We meet for teaching and encourage each believer to diligently engage in biblical studies. I prepare a teaching guide for every study along with relevant questions. A point of emphasis is shared to engage the learner into a viable discussion. Theological issues are raised, as well as theological reflection. Our aim is to see every believer grow into healthy believers. My model for teaching is to allow and encourage believers to ask questions and share insight for the good of the group. We grow disciples through love, intimacy, fellowship and encouragement, which means LIFE. We are discovering discipleship through experiencing God, a discipline study for examining a personal walk with God. We intend to use fifty days of love to spark interest in learning what it means to be genuine followers of Christ.

The church must encourage every believer to take the Great Commission seriously and to engage in the business of the whole counsel of Christian Discipleship. The church should care about making disciples because of the Great Commission. The Great Commission is the church's responsibility to the Divine Directive given by Christ.

The Sacred Art can be used for personal study as well as for groups. Its focus is to further pave the way and offer some fresh insights on discipleship as the church makes a rapid transition from tradition. *One insight is to help the church move away from business as usual.* Another insight is to *make disciples stronger, utilizing adequate and relevant resources.*

I conduct many seminars on leadership, stewardship and discipleship. I always keep my antennas up for fresh insights from others. No matter how busy the church gets involved in doing other things, there is always someone who really keeps focusing on growing healthy disciples. Even from the days of slavery, blacks have always had the desire to grow disciples. This was evident through the African American Experience. The African American church has always been the teaching institution in the community. In the African American church tradition, making disciples has always been a challenge, despite the experiences in the community as well as the social fabric of the community. There had been a lack of adequate resources in some churches to effectively develop disciples. As a result of these challenges, serious saints still pushed on. Regardless of the challenge, the pressing question is, Why Should The Church Care About Making Disciples? Well, making disciples can't be done without interaction. Interaction is necessary for growth. The church that cares about growing disciples is the church that totally follows the blueprint as designed by the master teacher, Jesus.

The church that cares really interacts with others. The eminent mystic theologian of the twentieth century, Howard Thurman, penned these veracious words: "We are aware of the circles that shut us in—cutting us off from each other. Despite our many–sided exposure to each other we are alone in our solitaries even in the midst of the congregation. Much of our aloneness is in the nature of things; much of it is due to the uncertainties or our own feelings about us and about others that make up the world of our familiars."[1]

I am in agreement with Dr. Thurman in that we, the church, the Body of Christ, have to do more and catch the vision that God has for us if we plan to effectively impact others for growth. We must get involved. In other words, kingdom building has to be on our minds, and we should strive to do more. There are many unchurched African Americans today, as well as others, and the challenge is to make a difference regarding individual discipleship. Teaching and training have been the catalyst of Christian education in the African American tradition. Individuals must have passion for helping others grow and to develop into healthy disciples. When I use the term "healthy" I am referring to those who are spiritually vibrant, energized, excited, firm and alert in the Word and living by faith. It is impossible to remain isolated in comfort zones that are not geared to helping the church in reaching its goal for making disciples. When we care about others, we care about them finding refuge in Christ as a key move. The church should set out to feed disciples, which will be discussed later.

Discipleship Investment

The task of developing disciples should be the church's main priority. It is an investment for kingdom purpose. Part of the task concerning discipleship is to admit shortcomings of the lack of knowledge that has demeaned our identity or role in church traditions, fundamental or conservative. In many churches of various traditions, there are those who are passionately fundamental about growing disciples. There are those who are conservative or liberal and have little claim on discipleship.

It is sad when the church overlooks and shirks her responsibility regarding discipling individuals for effective discipleship. While writing the *Sacred Art of Discipleship, some material grew out of the African American church.* I have wrestled with this material in workshops and teaching sessions at churches. I have changed the content of the material to really fit the personality of each church. Most times the change came during discussions, and the group provided insight. I believe that seven is a good number for a group. It is God's perfect number. It is suggested that three, or five, and also one on one are good numbers for a group.

Growing disciples is not limited to outside of the church,

but much work must be done within all of us. Many individuals have not a clue of what it means to be disciples. Before the church can do an outside job, it must do the inside job first. There is much work to be done on all of us. Jesus worked on His disciples as well as putting them to work.

For the purpose of emphasis and concern, the discipleship program in the African American church has for a long time been more in the context of Sunday school class. Weekly Bible study has been an asset for growing disciples. Many believers are trained from their church's denomination. They take classes and return to their church to teach others. Every pastor in the African American church tradition and other churches is challenged to grow new disciples.

There are many mainline and multi-cultural churches across America that has a viable discipleship program in full operation. They are nurturing believers and training them for their responsibilities. Salem Baptist Church of Chicago has a unique membership development ministry which trains new disciples. Christian Cultural Center of Brooklyn, New York, has a strong nurturing discipleship program. Saddleback Community Church, Lake Forest, California, trains believers from the beginning of their inception in the church to grow to become matured and responsible disciples with a purpose. West Angeles Church of God in Christ, Los Angeles, California has a strong discipleship program guiding lay Christians to maturity. Brooklyn Tabernacle, a multi-cultural church, grows disciples through prayer meetings. This is the first stage of intimacy. Believers are committed to mastering the concept of discipleship training as foundation to their Christian walk. As a result, the church is growing by leaps and bounds.

Introduction

The St. Paul Community Baptist Church, Brooklyn, New York, has a unique discipleship program for men. They are nurtured through teaching, dancing and drama.

The time has come for the real church to step forward and to become known to the world that she has the answer regarding reclaiming and reaffirming the lost ministry of discipleship. For too long, discipleship has been recessive in some churches. It has been a sleeping giant in the face of alert midgets. Midgets are classified as those who are underdeveloped and undernourished in the Word of God. Those who have midget mentalities think small and can't see at a distance. The purpose is to turn midgets into giants.

In one African American church I was conducting a teaching workshop. A deacon asked the question, "Which is more important leadership or discipleship? Many in the church are not willing of doing either." I thought that this was a good question to start our energy flowing. I attempted to answer disciples first. One can't be an effective leader without having gone through discipleship. Discipleship is first and leadership is second. They are hands–on entities for growing healthy churches. The person casually accepted my answer. The deacon was dealing with some issues. This means that the African American church has some issues to deal with while attempting to train new disciples. It is my belief that he was referring to the traditional form of leadership in the African American church rather than the greater responsibility of leadership connected to discipleship in contemporary form.

The ministry of discipleship is more important than traditional leadership. Traditional leadership does not fully prepare one for the battlefield, but discipleship does. The metaphor battlefield is where all of us are ministering. There is much opposition when we represent Jesus. The church can survive the battlefield because we are building on the foundation of Jesus. Every Christian is capable of being responsible through the right training.

Discipleship Vision

I believe that churches in the African American church tradition should take the responsibility of developing committed and healthy disciples. There is a need to have a vision for discipleship. The pastor must cast the vision and the church should follow. The church must understand certain tasks in growing disciples in order to be effective. Jesus had a vision for growing disciples. The Bible says, "Then he called the crowd to him along with his disciples and said: "If anyone would come after me, he must deny himself and take up his cross and follow me" (Mark 8:34). When Jesus calls, one must deny self and follow Jesus. Churches should have a *discipleship training program* that's designed to make disciples to become fishers of men. One cannot fish without knowing how to catch them. Catching requires skill. People are caught with the Word, prayer and faith.

- Understand that Christ taught His disciples as recorded from the Sermon on the Mount.
- Jesus sent His disciples out two by two.
- The early church modeled and implemented discipleship.
- The remainder of the New Testament models the gospels regarding making disciples.

Introduction

If churches will follow the above-suggested outline as one suggestion, then the church is at least heading in a positive direction and with preparation, there is no way to lose. Discipleship will come alive even in the midst of dry bones (see Ezekiel 37:1–17). I use dry bones as an example of starting from a depressive situation. What is needed is a discipleship resurrection. When the church is not making disciples, it is probably because there is no life in the valley and too much piety on the mountain. The primary objective of the healthy church is to sound the clarion call to invite people to come back to God. This means that the church must create ministries that meet the felt needs to liberate people. In order to get a better understanding of the above principles, I will refer more in detail in further chapters. The model for growing healthy disciples will transform churches from every walk of life, culture and ethnic group which will impact and make a change in communities.

I believe that believers will grow into being credible and viable disciples who will think theologically and develop their own *theology of ministry* that is biblically based. Now this will be the purpose and focus of chapter one.

STUDY REVIEW GUIDE: INTRODUCTION

Biblical Truth

Making disciples can't be done without interaction and commitment.

Key Word

DISCIPLE: The Greek word for disciple is *matheteuo,* which means in Matthew 28:19, in the active voice, being made a disciple.

Memory Verse

Mark 8:34

Point of Emphasis

Jesus really interacted with His disciples. He desired that they would learn.

Theological Reflection

Your theological views and reflection from this study.

Personal Application

Your thoughts on how this study has impacted you.

Study Questions

1. What is your understanding of discipleship?

2. How does your church understand discipleship?

3. How much do you think your church cares about discipleship?

4. How does the biblical truth relate to your ministry?

5. Why is it that some churches have fear of failure regarding discipleship?

PART 1

THE FOUNDATION FACTOR

Those who are interested in being genuine disciples of Christ have a desire to understand what it means to be a disciple and do what a disciple does. It also means to have a sure and strong foundation. This book is written to pastors and Christian education leaders. However, every Christian and every church can benefit from this study. My aim is to encourage believers who may be lax when it comes to discipleship to take it seriously. Before one can really be a true disciple, one must have a clear understanding of the nature and purpose of being a disciple. Ultimately, a disciple must connect and stay connected to Jesus.

Jesus was concerned that his followers would learn as much as they could. In Matthew 6:1–12 he took the time to teach them simple truths in the form of beatitudes. Teaching was His first love. We will journey, taking the time to use principles and approaches to describe what a disciple does and how the church can grow and be viable and responsible believers.

Discipleship is a practice in the church, guiding, leading and nurturing individuals for eternity with a strong foundation. In this study, the church at Philippi will serve as a major example for churches of all traditions, denominational and non-denominational.

1

A Sure Foundation

DEVELOPING A THEOLOGY OF DISCIPLESHIP

> "Another also said, I will follow You, Lord, and become Your disciple and side with Your party; but let me first say good-bye to those at my home. Jesus said to him, "No one who puts his hand to the plow and looks back [to the things behind] is fit for the kingdom of God." (Luke 9:61–62, The Message Bible)

Going with God requires total commitment.

There is a love fabric that exists in many churches across this nation and other countries. This love fabric is sacred, which is a prerequisite for having a strong faith and a sound theology. It takes love to really follow Jesus. One must be willing to go all the way for the glory of God. This is the basis for believing in Jesus. It is my desire to encourage churches to develop a theology of discipleship, while having the will to take bold steps for God. Taking bold steps is the basis for what and why one believes and does discipleship. Theology is the foundation for a sound discipleship ministry. Theology is the faith belief in God to guide the church through the phase of growing responsible disciples. I have wondered why many churches are too lax when it comes to really getting down to doing discipleship.

Too many churches sit and watch other churches march by with a viable program of Christian education geared for making disciples while they complain that we have never done it like that before, or they will say we don't have enough members or resources to make disciples. It is about total commitment. I have heard many leaders say that we are too small. Too small is the *midget mentality.* Is it either fear of success or fear of failure? If it's fear of success, it is probably because there are many traditional leaders who don't want to give up their spot. Many churches just don't think that they can offer a practical and reliable training on discipleship and this is why some churches have the fear of failure.

Until the churches recognize discipleship as priority, there will be no accountability for making disciples. The church will in no way be successful when the priority is unfocused. All true disciples are of the new birth and are developed later. The church's responsibility is to make them. Individuals through faith and the guidance of the Holy Spirit can be saved. However, we may present the plan of salvation, but it is the Holy Spirit that does the work. The church can't be afraid to make,

Part 1: The Foundation Factor

produce and duplicate disciples. Duplicating disciples means to train one to train another and so on and so on.

In many churches, there could be more excitement about growing disciples. To say the least, many churches are running over with new converts. They are going through training but are missing what it takes to disciples others. To answer the initial question regarding making disciples, many churches are right on target and do care about disciples. There are more churches in the south and other places that have a greater commitment for making disciples than in the northeast. I have heard the opinion from some pastors, "that in the south perhaps people seem to love the church more and in the northeast maybe people love the pastor more." Other areas in America could be different.

The church needs to make every effort count in growing disciples through nurture. Historically, as well as theologically, discipleship has been a challenging task for some churches and not so challenging for others. This is because I believe that some churches, pastors and Christian education leaders have mastered the art of disciple-making. There are committed mainline churches which maximize and implement the principles of the biblical model of disciple-making. As a pastor of an African American church, the African American church community has always upheld the fundamental teachings of Jesus and how His teachings connected to the Apostle Paul. Theology is deeply rooted in the African American experience. Before the infamous and renowned theologian James Cone, the leader in liberation theology, blacks had a theology of liberation. They believed God would deliver them from struggles.

It is possible that many churches will never reach the stage of being a disciple-making church. This is because too many other distractions are on the table. The commitment level is not there. What will happen is that some churches will claim disciple-making in name only. They will invite people to church and that's all they will do. It is more than inviting them to church.

Some churches are so eager and excited about new blood, that they will do what they can to increase the membership. Many of them get involved in organizations within the church, which have no focus for disciple-making. These organizations and clubs are concerned about their own agendas. These agendas have caused some churches to become trapped into traditional church trauma. Traditional church trauma is what I call a "blow to the local body." They are unconscious about disciple-making and too fearful to step out on faith.

When I hear many refer to the song, *"I am on the battlefield for my Lord, I am going to serve Him till I die"* means that there is no time for quitting and much more needs to be done. Growing disciples in the African American Church is like being on the battlefield. This is different from other church traditions. It is different because there are many oppositions which can impede progress and productivity. However, other church traditions do have oppositions as well. Those are some powerful lyrics, which I believe is discipleship theology, especially if one really believes it. The song is a faith song. There is the need for the church to show more faith in the line of duty. I am referring to a wider scope of responsibility that hinges on the church.

It is my hope that churches of all walks of life will ignite with the passion to make disciples. Many churches and denominations are on the decline in evangelizing the local communities and abroad. Before we can make disciples we must first go and get them. Jesus said in the Great Commission, "Go." Go means to move out and I will at this juncture offer some principles for going. I pray that every believer, church, witnessing team and denomination will have a passion to do the following, what I call the four W's of discipleship: *Witness to them,* w*in them, wait on them, and walk with them.* These are the major functions of making disciples.

Someone who presented the gospel to us first witnessed to us. This witnessing took us to another level because we were led by the work of the Holy Spirit. Jesus was patient with His disciples. He waited on them as they developed into healthy disciples. The church must have patience and wait on new converts to become mature disciples. Jesus walked with His disciples to give them direction and encouragement. New converts can't be turned loose and go by themselves; they need to know how to walk and where to walk. If they go out own their own too soon, they will become spiritually crippled. This is because they are not fully developed. Churches that are not afraid of making disciples must take the above with serious care in providing adequate training for disciples. The church is in need of dedicated Christian workers who are focused, motivated and ready to develop the harvest.

Training Ground for Disciples

The disciple-making process is a process of commitment and dedication which was first started by Jesus. This means that discipleship is God-centered and Christ-focused. When Jesus called the disciples at the Sea of Galilee, he called them for a lifetime. A lifetime commitment is to follow Him. "Come, follow me," Jesus said, "and I will make you fishers of men" (Mark 1:17). This verse is identified as the sacred call, which is the call to commitment, the call to dedication and the call to responsibility and a call to risk. True disciples must be willing to take risks. One must be willing to be criticized for identifying with Christ. All of the above is part of basic training for Christian discipleship. Churches must really believe that Jesus called the church to this ministry.

Pastors of all churches must encourage people to value discipleship. This is the central core of the life of the church. This means without a clear program and plan for doing discipleship, the religious life of the church will suffer. Most American Churches do not have a clear understanding of what it means to do discipleship. Every believer has a calling to be a genuine disciple. Discipleship has always been viewed or accepted as the sacred art, but little focus has been given to growing disciples in churches of different faiths and denominations. Pastors and lay leaders in the church who had the vision for building new disciples did it the best they knew how.

The Sea of Galilee was the initial starting point of evangelism. Evangelism is a strong component of discipleship, but it is not discipleship. However, discipleship and evangelism go hand in hand. Evangelism is reaching out and witnessing and discipleship is nurturing, teaching and training. Growing disciples is an urgent matter! Jesus does the calling through the unction and ministry of the Holy Spirit. When Jesus called them by the Sea of Galilee, He called them to quit what they were doing and to live a life of faith as disciples. They were great fishers in their own vocation. Not only were the disciples committed to disciple-making, but the Early Church as well. Jesus was preparing His disciples for Christian leadership.

When one accepts Christ as personal Savior, the calling of discipleship begins. The church can make more disciples when there is an understanding that discipleship is the foundation when one accepts Christ as Lord. After the acceptance comes the assignment. Christ never assigned anyone until they knew what they were going to do. One of the fallacies of the modern day church is that so many individuals have tried to take assignments and tasks ill prepared. In order for the church to really make disciples, it is suggested that one takes a serious look at how Jesus interacted with and how He communicated to His disciples.

The church needs the zest and the zeal to keep the focus on the Great Commission. Individuals who have focus will not quit until the entire church sees the vision. There are too many other distractions, which distorts the vision of the church to focus on the all-important ministry of the church. When a disciple becomes focused, he or she becomes a spiritual asset to the ministry of discipleship.

The pastor, who is the servant leader of the church, should set the stage for such important emphasis. "Successful pastors care about the discipleship commitment of their people, they monitor it closely and they respond when the numbers suggest a waffling of dedication to spiritual advancement."[2] This means that discipleship must be prayed up, preached about and taught on. I think it would be a good idea to have a banner up in the church reminding the church of Matthew 28:18–20, the Great Commission. It will also be helpful to keep it in the church's bulletin, newsletters, and bumper stickers. We should promote and encourage the church to see the big picture for making disciples, which will be explained in detail in the chapters to come.

Discipleship and Faith

In many churches, discipleship and faith have been in the same context of learning. They have not been diametrically opposed to each other. To be a strong disciple, one needed to have faith. For African Americans, faith grew out of the slave tradition. For the slaves, the focus was being able to see Christ in the diverse context of their experience. The diverse context of faith was tough and challenging. It was ever before them, and then they had less fear of failure. They knew what Christ expected. Before the church can really keep focused, the church needs to make a commitment to two goals, *prayer and faith.* Churches from various walks of life can identify with faith in their own experience and their discipleship. The following prayer is a prayer for encouragement for churches and individuals.

Disciple-Making Prayer: Eternal God we, the church, come before your awesome presence to thank you for having organized us as a recognized body of baptized believers, for the sole purpose of building your kingdom. We ask that you give us the desire, the passion and patience to make disciples. I am borrowing a prayer line from the African American tradition: "Lord you may not come when we want you but you are always on time." Thank You God for not letting our beds be our cooling board." We do not have the answers but you do. Lead us through the Holy Spirit as we minister through praying, counseling, preaching and teaching. Help us to be faithful and true to your mandate as we lead others to green pastures and fresh meadows so that they may experience you fully as true disciples, growing and maturing. We pray in your name, Amen.

Faith: All believers need faith in order to be true disciples. "But without faith no one can please God. We must believe that God is real and that he rewards everyone who searches for him." (Hebrews 11:6, CEV). Individuals are moved when they see faith working in and through leaders. Having faith in God keeps the church focused on helping to fulfill the mandate of the Great Commission. A theology of discipleship in the church is a theology of survival and a theology of hope. All believers need a theology of survival and a theology of hope.

Keeping the church focused on the Great Commission is a task. It is incumbent upon the leadership of the church to keep this mandate alive. This process involves teamwork. It takes more than one person to convince and persuade the saints of God to keep the emphasis alive. The church will be successful when teaching and training is in perspective. Every seminar, class, workshop, Bible study group and even sermons from the pulpit should keep the theme of *nurturing disciples* constantly on the agenda.

The focus of the Great Commission should be the total work of the church. When new converts are brought to the church, they should be indoctrinated on the Great Commission with a clear understanding of the focus of the Great Commission. The more that is taught, the more the church becomes interested in seeing this ministry take flight in the church. I hope that churches change their focus from omission to commission and begin to see the big picture of what it really means to be identified as genuine followers of Christ.

Staying Ready

As part of developing a theology of discipleship, field work is needed. Jesus was always available for His disciples when they needed Him. No matter what the situation was, Jesus showed up at the stated time. Jesus said, "And surely I am with you always, to the very end of the age" (Matthew 28:20). Just as Jesus was available, he taught the disciples to be available. He guided them in every phase of their work.

Disciples must be available to win and witness to those who are held captive and need to be set free. Disciples can't do any evangelism unless he or she is available. Available means to be ready for the task which is at hand. Those disciples who have been properly nurtured were ready to take charge of their own discipleship responsibility. Jesus trained his disciples to go to the surrounding areas. They were available to go to Jerusalem, Decapolis, Cana of Galilee, Bethany, Samaria, Judea and Caesarea.

In some instances and in many churches, discipleship was not born because evangelism was trapped and cornered in the tradition of the church, therefore, hindering the church to be obedient to the Great Commission. Those who are loyal to tradition have a "weak theology," which is marked by a low keyed disciple-making process. A strong faith is needed to call the church to total commitment.

Every church and every believer must have a theological

understanding of discipleship as well as a doctrine of God. A doctrine of God is simply an individual's understanding about what has been taught and what he or she believes about the nature and existence of God. Everyone does not have the same doctrine about God, but they will have many similarities. It is important to help veteran believers as well as new believers to think theologically. Thinking theology is not only for the academy, but for the church as well. However, seminaries encourage divinity students to make the best of their three years of study and to develop their theology based on the Bible, faith and their church tradition. It is important for the church to be a strong advocate of theology. Having a theology of discipleship adds credibility to ones' witness. Each ministry group should discuss the significance of understanding theology. Jesus certainly taught His disciples to have a doctrine of God. He wanted to know how they felt about Him and who they thought he was (Matthew 16:18).

If churches do not become committed and adequately nurture disciples, then the church will be guilty of producing non-disciples. As a minister of the gospel, I am dedicated to the task of sharing the ministry of discipleship development. I invite other churches and pastors to light the candle and let the light shine, set the stage and implement justice for setting the captives free. This leads to what I will talk about in chapter two.

THE SACRED ART

DIAGRAM 1

The Foundation for Discipleship
A Church-Centered Theological Plan

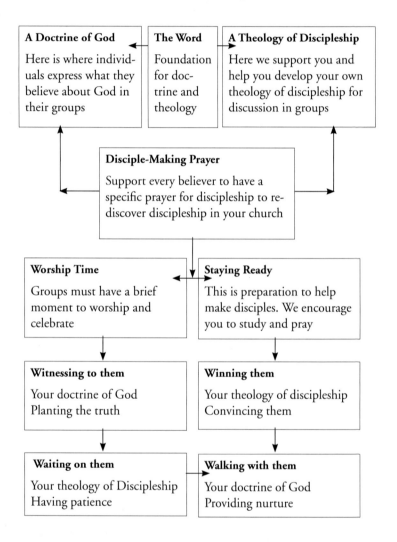

STUDY REVIEW GUIDE: A SURE FOUNDATION

Biblical Truth

It takes a lifetime commitment to follow Jesus.

Key Word

FOLLOW: The Greek word for follow is *akoloutheo*, which means "one going in the same way."

Memory Verses

Mark 1:16–18

Point of Emphasis

It is important to have a deep theological view of discipleship.

Theological Reflection

Your theological views and reflection from this study.

Personal Application

Your thoughts on how this study has impacted you.

Study Questions

1. Why is it necessary for the church to have a theological view of discipleship?

2. Why is a strong faith needed to call the church to total commitment?

3. Why is it important to value discipleship?

4. How does the biblical truth relate to your ministry?

5. What is the connection between evangelism and discipleship, and what is their major difference?

A Strong Foundation

Understanding the Biblical Plan of Discipleship for God's Church

> Then Jesus came to them and said, "All authority in heaven and on earth has been given to me. Therefore go and make disciples of all nations, baptizing them in the name of the Father and of the Son and of the Holy Spirit, and teaching them to obey everything I have commanded you. And surely I am with you always, to the very end of the age." (Matthew 28:18–20)

Following the Biblical plan of discipleship is necessary. The basis for the biblical plan of discipleship is stated here in the Great Commission. It is in these verses that Christ lifts up the sacred art of discipleship as the foundation for building healthy disciples. Churches must advocate efforts to build healthy disciples for the glory of God. However, some churches have stronger discipleship programs than others. Therefore, Jesus' purpose was to make discipleship the central focus. Doing discipleship is the epitome of what Christ expects His church to be. In order for the church to be obedient to God, she must have a clear understanding of the biblical plan of discipleship.

Jesus sets the record straight after the eleven disciples meandered their way to Galilee to the mountain appointed by Jesus. God gave Jesus the divine authority to commission the disciples for service. Discipleship ministries must be centered on the biblical plan of discipleship. The biblical plan of discipleship is fivefold: (1) The church is commanded to go (2) The church is commissioned to make disciples. (3) The church is commissioned to baptize. (4) The church is commissioned to teach and (5) The church is commissioned to have a watchful eye, observing all things.

The church would be effective in fulfilling its commission when it is clear that God has given direction to go. The danger is going before God gives the signal. The signal comes in the name of the Father, the Son and the Holy Spirit. Christians must take the commission seriously. This means that every believer is a disciple and that the church is made up of disciples. A disciple cannot engage in discipleship without first having an understanding of the plan, purpose and focus of discipleship.

Too many churches are at the crossroads of their ministry, wondering why their church is not as attractive as it should be, attractive in the sense of having something unique to offer that is appetizing, fulfilling, and promising. One reason for this unattractiveness is a lack of focus and purpose. People need to be nurtured and edified as disciples. I mean, why are so many parishioners not as strong in the faith? The ministry of the individual and the church is crippled, because many believers are not living as responsible disciples.

Consequently, many churches are losing parishioners because they have not really found their rightful place in the Body of Christ. They are not doing much and are not going anywhere. The answer is that individuals, who have not made discipleship a prime emphasis, have weakened the focus on discipleship.

Discipleship has missed its focus because its significance has been underestimated. Many are going in the opposite direction instead of forward because of disobedience. This disobedience has been a disadvantage to the ministry and mandate of making disciples. It is simply ridiculous to blame the pulpit for the entire ministry of discipleship. Discipleship is not territorial to the ordained ministry; it is to be shared by the laity as well. The entire church must merge to motivate and inspire others to break out of their comfort zones and help to effectively disciple others. Too many Christians have been laminated with pride, frustrated with fear, and stitched in arrogance to even talk with someone about their eternal destiny.

The church today is filled with many underdeveloped and undernourished disciples. We are sitting on the cutting edge of the millennium and are now stepping into a new realm of time. The spirit of complaining and complacency is outdated, and though we can't make up for lost time, we can do our best with the time that is left. We should "redeem the time because the days are evil" (Ephesians 5:16, NKJV). There is no time to waste. The church must take a more serious role in adequately preparing for harvest and provide spiritual food for needy, undernourished individuals. I am reminded of a classic hymn of the church which says: *"what can make me whole again, nothing but the blood of Jesus."* The power of the blood is a continuous process by which one develops and grows into spiritual maturity. There must be an allegiance of discipleship faith because of what God did for us in Christ. John states that, "For this is the love of God, that we keep His commandments." His commandments are not burdensome. "For whatever is born of God overcomes the world, and this is the victory that overcomes the faith. Who is he who overcomes the world, but he who believes that Jesus is the Son of God?" (1 John 5:3–6, NKJV).

Discipleship is the extended work of the disciple. Therefore, the work is never exhausted. There are twenty-nine passages in the New Testament which specifically deal with discipleship. I will refer to a portion of these for this study since all of the scriptures are contextually in the same biblical unity. The emphasis points to learning and applying what the teacher teaches.

The biblical context of discipleship is contextually taught in these passages: Matthew 9:14, 10:1, 22:16, Luke 22:11 and John 8:31. The purpose of the church is to clearly understand and bring discipleship to center stage for a viable witness. Renowned father and son team Arn Win and Charles Win clarify that Christ expects every disciple to be a witness. Witnessing to the good news is simply the expression of Christian discipleship. Acts 1:8 provides an important key to Christ's expectations of His disciples. Jesus said, "You shall be My witnesses."[3] No matter what and how others view the church, a disciple is for life (Matthew 10:22). The church through the discipleship ministry must provide matchless service unto the end without wavering. This means that the church must have a tenacious spirit for instilling and advocating the ministry of redemptive fellowship. Every church should focus on helping the lost to become redeemed.

The Biblical Roles of Disciples?

Every disciple must know without reservation or equivocation his or her duty to Christ and the church. Each disciple must fulfill a specific role as outlined in the Scriptures. Each function is distinctive in character.

1. *Disciples are Servants*

A disciple is not greater than his or her master (see Matthew 10:24). Disciples can become better when they serve with their heart. In addition, serving becomes effective when there is a clear understanding of the meaning of a servant disciple. The New Testament word for servant is *Doulos,* and refers to one being in bondage. The image of slave in the New Testament is identified in the African American Tradition. A disciple really does the comprehensive work of Christ. A servant must provide service, and that's why the word *Diakonos,* the basic Greek word for service is used. In essence, it is one who ministers. One cannot honestly minister without serving. They go hand-in hand. A servant is one who has passion for others without any strings attached. This means that a servant, clergy or laity is not satisfied until someone is helped.

Churches, pastors, lay leaders and other parishioners should be at the beckoning call and provide five-star service to individuals and families. When one comes to church, they should be so impressed that they can't wait until the next time. Don't provide service that will run people away, give them the best and minister to their needs with compassion and pride.

2. Disciples are Believers

Discipleship becomes null and void without believing. Everything else about a disciple hinges on the fact that they are believers in Christ Jesus. There is no pretending or camouflaging. True discipleship will show up in our daily commitment. The Christian walk and talk centers on the practice and faith message of the Bible. Jesus said, "Whoever believes and is baptized will be saved, but he who does not believe will be condemned" (Mark 16:16). Believers are really another way of saying true followers. Jesus is looking for believers who will be loyal to Him in everything they set out to do. Believers belong to the family of God. Belonging to the family of God is a sacred privilege, because it offers a divine endowment of blessings. Being a believer means that one must implement what he or she believes about Christ in a practical way that pleases God.

3. Disciples are Learners

We as believers cannot ever get enough instruction. When the opportunity avails itself for learning, we should seize the moment. No one can give adequate excuse that he or she can't find a place to learn more about the Word of God. There are many schools in which one can take courses to become better equipped. However, it is important to inquire about a particular school regarding its quality and validity of the truth. James says that we should "study to show yourself approved, a workman unto God rightly dividing the word of truth" (II Tim 2:15). The more we learn, the more we have to share with others concerning the deep things of God. There is never enough time to learn as much about the Word of God. Every disciple must put forth the effort to understand the scriptures and apply them accordingly.

4. *Disciples are Followers*

Disciples are also followers of Christ. This means that being a disciple as a follower of Christ is to follow all the way. Members of the family of God has for over centuries followed Jesus. There are ten words for follow in the Greek. It is too exhaustive to examine all these words in this study. In this context, the word "follow" means companion, which means unity. This word is in this form *for* discipleship. The word "follow" is from the Greek word *akoloutheo*, which means a follower or a disciple. Other forms of Greek words are used differently *for* the word "follow." *Epakoloutheo* is a companion to *akoloutheo*, which means to follow after, keep going. Both forms of the words specifically refer to a disciple.

It is impossible to be a real disciple without following Jesus. Jesus called his disciples to go to work and to go to work by fishing *for* souls *for* Christ. They followed Him *from* Galilee, Decapolis, Jerusalem, Judea and beyond Jordan (Matthew 4:25). We are to follow Jesus and do as He says. He gives us the guide and direction and we are to follow it with sincerity. We are not on our own; we are dependent upon God as

His followers. When we truly follow Him, we are true to His Word. Following Him means to do exactly that, follow Him. Under no circumstances, are we to get ahead of Him.

5. Disciples are Proclaimers/Evangelists

One cannot be a true disciple without sharing God's Word with others. There are churches in all denominations and non-denominations that are adamant regarding the proclamation of the Word. One of the worst things in any church tradition is to be guilty of not sharing the Word. It is not solely left up to the preacher/pastor to spread the Word. The word "proclaim" comes from the Greek word *kerusoo*, which means to proclaim or preach. In Acts 8:5 "Phillip went down to Samaria and preached Christ to them." Phillip was not an ordained preacher, but a deacon. He preached with power and confidence. He was not afraid to share the gospel. The word "proclaim" in this context means that every disciple should be able to share the Word of God. They have to be trained and trained beyond their fears.

A course in Apologetics is necessary when disciples have reached the advanced stage of their training. Apologetics has to do with being able to defend Christianity when presenting the gospel. Disciples are proclaimers; they are to share the plan of salvation, which is the proclamation process. Bill Hull states, "Every Christian should be trained how to verbalize the Gospel."[4] This is necessary for the effectiveness of the gospel. When the laity really learn how to present the gospel, both discipleship and evangelism will leave its marks in the hearts of individuals and change them forever.

6. Disciples are Team Players

The church's task is too great and too vast for one or two to do all of the work. The mission of the church carries with it the burden of being overwhelming. One will be challenged to enter the mission field. The bottom line is that the church needs help. Jesus sent disciples out two by two. This was done for confirmation, that others would see what God can do through discipleship teams. The church should seek to fulfill the mission of discipleship by involving as many as possible working together. Discipleship is authentic when the entire church is at work.

7. *The Major Assignment for Disciples*

God has the answer to our direction, mission and ministry. We cannot assign ourselves to any task or mission. We may have a desire to go some place, but it is totally left up to God to give us clearance. As disciples, we have a major assignment, and that assignment is outlined in the gospel of Luke as the Christ's Commission. Jesus called His disciples and endowed them with power and authority over all demons and diseases. He sent them on a preaching and healing mission (Luke 9:1–6). God will give us many other assignments. Many of them are, as Blackaby calls them, "God-sized assignments."[5] The churches of all faith traditions have had many God–sized assignments. Those assignments are difficult and really test one's faith. They are more than one can envision, so it takes a miracle of faith to see God at work. God-sized assignments are assigned by God for every situation that needs attention. Jesus was the only one who could handle God-sized assignments.

Jesus confronts the Samaritan woman regardless of gender or culture. The emphasis of the conversation is that God knows more about where we should be. It is important that we make every effort to make a discipleship contact. Walter A. Hemichsen states that "Jesus did not push the Samaritan woman. He engaged her in conversation and allowed her to ponder the implications of what has been said. As you read through the story, you notice that salvation became her idea, not just His. She ended up truly wanting it. He did not push it on her."[6]

Making a disciple was more important than culture, class or gender. There was much hatred between Jews and Samaritans, very similar to whites and blacks, and any other minority group. Jesus' mission was to cut through the rubbish of bitterness amid hatred and bring peace. He was making preparation to go to Jerusalem. He was not going without having firsthand knowledge of what it was to be rejected. He was ready for his God-sized assignment at Jacob's well. Today the church cannot afford to overlook and fail to witness to others who are of a different culture, even where there is hatred, bitterness or anger. The problem with many churches today is that they are passing by Jacob's well. Jacob's well could be your co-worker sitting next to you at work, on a plane, or on the assembly line at the manufacturing plant, or wherever there is contact.

The assignment for discipleship is a serious endeavor in churches that have been lax regarding discipleship. It is serious because it requires total commitment and dedication for such a task in such a hostile world. As we enter the throes of this world and the communities in which we live, we will need the blessing of God to give us unction for such a task. There is no doubt that when Jesus sends out disciples, they

PART 1: THE FOUNDATION FACTOR

are sent with what it takes to do ministry. When Jesus met the women at the well, while he ministered to her, he sent His disciples into the city to buy food (John 4:7–8). Disciples are not disciples just to sit and do nothing. There is much work to be done. We must not underestimate our assignment.

The action plan for discipleship precedes the New Testament. Discipleship carries various meanings, those in the Old Testament were followers, learners, proclaimers, servants, believers, team players and dedicated to the work of God. The prophets of old were individuals of prayer and faith. Abraham had an abundance of faith. In Genesis, God told Abraham, "The LORD had said to Abraham, 'Leave your country, your people and your father's household and go to the land I will show you'" (Genesis 12:1). He went without knowing where he would end up. He was obedient to God. He left totally on his faith. Disciples must have faith, be obedient and listen to God. God knows more about where we should be than we would ever know. Abraham, Moses and Aaron were team players. They were servants to the people. God had trusted the Israelites in their hands. God gave Moses his first lesson on Mt. Sinai. God drilled Moses in the Ten Commandments (Exodus 20:1–17). They were doing discipleship work when they crossed over the Red Sea. This was a God-sized assignment. The people became impatient with Moses because he stayed too long on Mt. Sinai, and as a result, they desired to listen to Aaron (Exodus 32:1–10).

David was another example of one who was close to God. In the Old Testament, the action plan was to follow obedience in all areas of life. God blessed through obedience. It is clear that Jesus has a plan for His disciples. The first step for the action plan is to identify the problem. Jesus knew that there were problems all around Him, and no one wanted to hear. He had an *action plan* for everything He did with His disciples. We shall take a look at these biblical action plans.

The First Plan of Action Is To Call. Jesus called them and told them to follow Him (Matthew 4: 18–22). The church can't call disciples, but can surely pick them up and nurture them by inviting them to church for training and development. The call of discipleship is not limited to any one location, but a wide area of ministry. The Master did not call them to stay in one location. According to Robert E. Coleman, "the initial objective of Jesus' plan was to enlist men who could bear witness to his work after he returned to the father. John and Andrew were the first to be invited as Jesus left the scene of the great revival of the Baptist at Bethany beyond the Jordan (John 1:35–40)."[7] Today, Jesus enlists both men and women to continue the work that he started.

Responding to the call of discipleship is getting ready for a greater ministry that will impact lives and make a difference regardless of race, culture or gender. Coleman is right on target in that Jesus prepared disciples to bear witness of his work. The church must have an intentional plan and purpose for recruiting and training individuals to do ministry.

The Second Plan of Action Was To Teach Them. (Matthew (5:1–12). There is no substitution for teaching saints. Where there is no teaching there is no nurture. "As new born babes desire the sincere milk *of* the word" (1 Peter 2:2). Later I will address Paul's thought on growing up through teaching. There is no escape *from teaching* if the church plans to stay in the will of God. In some churches, there is much entertainment. Many love to take the role *of showmanship.* They love to do other things more than being involved in teaching. As much as pastors and other leaders in churches encourage people to become involved in teaching and training, many reject the idea. Some feel that they know it all, or they feel that some can't even teach them. The emphasis in this plan is to help others to see the need for on-going teaching and training.

The Third Plan of Action Was Prayer. (Matthew 6:5–13). Oppositions come in many forms and circumstances. This part of the action plan is highly authenticated in the African American Church. The African American Church seriously believes in prayer. I refer to the African American Church because of such a rich and religious heritage. There are other churches, and multi-cultural churches that strongly implement prayer among believers. However, believers in all communities pray more than others. These believers know the word of prayer. Prayer is the link to the heartbeat of God facilitating righteousness in the lives of disciples through the operation and unction of the Holy Spirit. It is an intimate contact with God who knows our every concern. We must be able to talk to God when things are well, and when things are not so well. Jesus included time in His ministry to talk with God. No matter what He did, or planned to do, He prayed. Prayer is the soul's entrance into the presence of the Almighty. Prayer is our spiritual vitamins for daily nutrients which keeps us healthy. Prayer is God's protection in the presence of evil. The emphasis and purpose is to pray, pray, and pray.

The Fourth Plan of Action was Fasting. Fasting goes hand-in hand with prayer. Every disciple needs to fast as much as possible. Jesus fasted forty days and forty nights in preparation of His public ministry (Matthew 4:2). Every believer should model his or her spiritual life after Christ. Our Savior spent these days totally alone with His father. He had to prepare for his years as He ministered in towns and villages. Fasting may cause the physical body to become weak and tired because of a lack of food, but it provides strength for the soul. It is spiritual cleansing and sets the tone for what lies ahead. If every believer would take fasting seriously before starting their ministry, they will definitely have spiritual resources to combat the forces of evil and sadistic oppositions. It is a guarantee that various oppositions will come and challenge the household of faith. One must be brave and bold to defy the attacks on the church by a secular society that has no discipleship purpose.

The Fifth Plan of Action Was Power Over Unclean Spirits. The real test of discipleship is to know when unwanted or unclean spirits are in reach. Every disciple of Christ must be endowed with the Holy Spirit. The Holy Spirit is our supporter in the context of giving us power over unclean spirits. It is impossible for the church to nurture and make disciples without being bold and brave. Disciples can't be afraid of unclean spirits. Jesus confronted His disciples for being faithless in casting out demons. "Oh faithless and perverse generation, how long shall I be with you? How long shall I bear with you? Bring him here to Me" (Matthew 17: 17, NKJV). The church cannot allow unclean spirits to take control of the disciples. If they do, the ministry of discipleship becomes weak and ineffective. The context of this phase of the action plan is to keep demons from attacking disciples. The church must use the power that God has given. The anointing power of the Holy Spirit is the weapon of warfare. Too many are unfocused, and this is when the attack can and will be detrimental to the health of the Body of Christ.

The Biblical Mandate for Disciples?

This is a critical moment in the life of all churches. There are so many competitive things, which distract believers in every local church. When we examine the role of a disciple, we examine what a disciple should do. Every believer should have a plan of doing whatever God has gifted him or her to do. Since we are followers of Jesus, he has left great examples in the New Testament for us to follow. Marcus Borg says, "Yet the mighty deeds of Jesus are also part of the history of Jesus, and not simply part of church's *story about* Jesus. That, is the tradition that Jesus was a "wonder-worker" is historically very firmly attested."[8] The way in which a disciple acts affects the growth of the church is in two ways. The first is an unforgiving heart. The eyes of the world are on the church. No matter what the church does, there is going to be criticisms.

Believers should not allow the spirit of unforgiveness to linger, because it will add to an unhealthy relationship with Christ and a negative relationship with others. Jesus in the Sermon on the Mount makes reference to the law of reconciliation. It is important that believers reconcile their differences and forgive each other before praying to God (Matthew 5:23–26). This unhealthy relationship robs individuals of joy and happiness in the Holy Spirit. In reality, one's testimony will have little authority.

The second act is showing a lack of love. God is love and

we must show love to each other. I Corinthians chapter 13 is the love chapter of the Bible. It must be studied and applied and implemented. The church grows as the individual grows in the Word. The third act is showing humility. The Apostle Paul clearly addresses the issue of how a disciple should act as found in (Philippians 2:1–11). These verses epitomize the character of the Christian life. Christ is the prime example of showing humility. Therefore, every believer must think like Christ. Although Paul does not use the term disciple, he refers to the general term Christian for disciple. His emphasis is Christological. Let us look at four principles in regard to this passage:

1. The Mark of Humility

2. Disciples Should Think Like Christ

3. Disciples Should be Obedient

4. Disciples Must take a Stand

The Mark of Humility

It is impossible to be true to God the Father, God the Son and God the Holy Spirit without being humble. It is unhealthy for disciples to walk around with insensitive feelings. Humility is the result of a compassionate spirit. It is important to be submissive. It is not a sign of weakness, but meekness. There is nothing that can be substituted for humility. Every disciple has the responsibility to reach out and help others. When we think about it, every disciple is humble. If one is not humble, then, he or she is not really a true disciple. Humbleness comes with the new birth. As described in John 3:1–21, believers or disciples have a new life in Christ because they have been born with the spirit. So therefore, there is a divine responsibility to be to be humble. Leaders in the church should practice humility in every phase of church life. Disciples must live a life of humility. Disciples make up churches and churches make up associations, and associations make up conventions. These entities must know the importance of the nature of humility. When this happens, the ministry of discipleship will encourage all believers to strive to make disciples.

Disciples Should Think like Christ

The way a disciple thinks, charts the course of his or her spiritual journey. After spiritual birth, every disciple should think about spiritual things. One really cannot think like the world, act like the world and be a true disciple. The Apostle Paul challenges every believer to have a mind like Christ. The Apostle Paul says, "Your attitude should be the same as that of Christ Jesus" (Philippians 2:5). Paul succinctly states that every believer must adopt the ways of Christ. Every believer must encourage other believers to think like Christ. It's the only way to becoming fruitful for winning individuals for the kingdom. William Barclay notes that, "Jesus won the hearts of men, not by blasting them with power, but by showing them a love they could not resist."[9] If a church doesn't practice the ways of Christ, then that church's discipleship program will have a dry spell. When the church's ministry is dry, it cannot inspire anyone to follow leadership to develop and mature as believers. Christ kept His disciples asking questions. He taught them to act and think like Him. Every church must set the stage for training disciples to think like Christ and encourage new disciples to be active participants rather than bench members. Churches must always have something to offer. Training and motivating disciples to think like Christ keeps the church on target for making more disciples. This is implementing the Great Commission.

Disciples Should be Obedient

There is nothing worse than being disobedient. Disobedient disciples and churches are those who do not carry out the function of disciple-making. Disobedience is when there is no witnessing. Churches that are serious and conscious of the work of God will always have on its agenda a viable plan for reaching and developing new disciples. Reaching and developing new disciples is not just left to the pastor, but it includes every believer. There are too many times when pastors are blamed when the church is not growing. There is a misconception or myth that the pastor has only been selected to evangelize and develop disciples. As said earlier, discipleship is for the entire church. It is a team effort for both the pulpit and the pew.

Disciples Must Stand on Their Own feet

When disciples are able to take a stand, they are showing good stewardship. A genuine disciple is an excellent steward. They both go hand-in hand. *Jesus* left His disciples in good hands. He left them with the Holy Spirit as recorded in John 16:7–15. Disciples can't stand on their feet unless the Holy Spirit guides them. He was preparing them for His eminent return to the Father. He prepared them because He knew what they would have to face in their ministries. Every believer must be courageous in order to fulfill the Master's plan of discipleship. In order for disciples to stand on their feet, they have to be in the Word and walk accordingly to its principles. Jesus had a seven-fold discipleship plan designed to ensure church growth. *(See Diagram 2)*

Diagram 2

A Seven-fold Church-Based Discipleship Plan

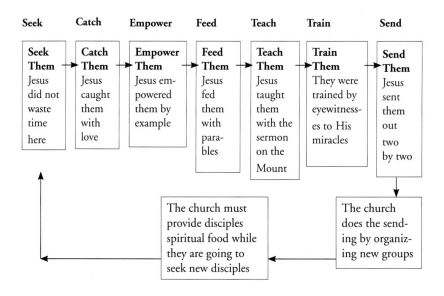

Every church must seriously examine the phases that Jesus took His disciples through to adequately prepare them to do His work. It is necessary to be consistent in moving people to seek others in a continuous direction. It is necessary to adopt and implement Jesus' seven-fold discipleship plan. Churches can definitely develop a more detailed plan conducive to their training program. The church based-discipleship plan is explained in the following manner, we are to:

1. Seek Them This stage of discipleship is to seek them. It is perhaps the most difficult stage. It was not difficult for Jesus. Jesus had a definite goal and a selected group of followers. In the aggressive phase, Jesus wasted no time in going after His disciples. The church must plan ahead and set things in order with a purpose like Jesus. Jesus knew what they were doing for a living. He had a plan for them as well as a promise. He passed alongside the Sea of Galilee and called them from their fishing vocations to follow Him. Churches must have assertive workers ready to seek for Jesus' work. We have many Sea of Galilee's today. Just look around, people are everywhere. The U.S. Census report is increasing. There are many unemployed people in the church who have not used their skills and gifts for the ministry. The church today and tomorrow will have to follow Jesus on pure faith.

2. Catch Them This stage of discipleship is the most challenging, because the goal is to be able to catch people. When disciples are caught, this is the patience phase. Jesus was not in such a hurry that he overlooked the twelve. He knew that kindness and love would win them. This is a critical phase in the discipleship plan. It is critical because people could be caught. Jesus wants us to go to church, but he wants the church to go after new and prospective disciples. Jesus instructed His disciples who were fishing how to fish right. They were fishing all night and had not caught anything. There nets were on the wrong side of the ship. When they took Jesus' advice, they caught a multitude of fish. In the same passage in Luke, Jesus commissioned the disciples to fish for men (Luke 5: 1–10). What the church needs to do is cast the net on the other side of the ship. The other side of the ship is uncharted waters, valleys, mountains and hills. It is any place when people are waiting.

3. Empower Them This stage of discipleship is to empower them. After disciples are caught, the church can't leave them to sit idle because idleness leads to illness. When disciples are not busy doing positive things, they become weakened in their faith and ineffective. Jesus empowered His disciples by examples. He showed them how to take charge and how to drive out unclean spirits. Unclean spirits will be discussed in another chapter. This phase teaches that every disciple must have power in order to function effectively in this phase.

4. Feed Them This stage of discipleship is to feed them. This stage is closely associated with being empowered. Jesus used parabolic illustrations to make the truth stick and everyday situations clear in relation to heavenly meaning. When parables were used, the disciples were motivated and encouraged. The use of parables permeated and radiated the soul. Their souls were fed to the highest. Wholesome feeding is the first sign of sound leadership. If they are fed, they will follow. When new converts are fed the Word of God, they are fed the right food. A new believer can't absorb too much at one time. They need to be nurtured slowly. It takes time for new believers to develop to being responsible disciples. Jesus told Peter to feed His sheep, "When they had finished eating, Jesus said to Simon Peter, "Simon son of John, do you truly love me more than these?" "Yes, Lord," he said, "you know that I love you." Jesus said, "Feed my lambs" (John 21:15). Jesus told peter three time to feed his sheep. He wanted to make sure peter understood the request. The church must follow Jesus' example and make provision for each disciple.

5. Teach Them This stage of discipleship is foundational. A strong foundation is a foundation for life. In Jesus' Sermon on the Mount, He thought it was necessary to make it clear by teaching." Then He opened His mouth and taught them" (Matthew 5:2). The difference between parables and the Sermon on the Mount is that parables were methods to explain, whereas the Sermon on the Mount teaches lessons for life. Jesus said, "Blessed are the poor in spirit, for theirs is the kingdom of heaven" (Matthew 5:3). This means that individuals were guaranteed a place in heaven. He just did not leave them there. People came from far and near because they have not heard such powerful words before.

6. Training Them This stage of discipleship is really getting ready for the challenge. Training shows one how to do what needs to be done. Jesus took His disciples on every mission. He wanted them to experience His miracles that He performed. They were on the job training in the apex of Jesus' public ministry. An example of training is found in Mark 14:22–25 on the Institution of the Lord's Supper. He was preparing to leave them. He trained them for everything they had to do. When training is done, it makes a statement that a church takes discipleship seriously. It is moving training to center stage, which is an important objective of the ministry of Christian education.

7. Send Them This stage of discipleship is to send them. In this stage, Christ expected His disciples to be prepared to go. In order to make disciples, the church must commission them and send them to make disciples.

After all, He had taught them efficiently for the task. It is not good for churches to send disciples out alone, but in pairs. In addition, when they go out they must be on the same page. There is no time for guessing or blundering. This is no time to be seen. It is no time to make impressions. It is discipleship time. That is the time to really stay focused and keep the discipleship process going. Jesus sent disciples out in groups of two. Sending refers to a specific mission. "Then Jesus went around teaching from village to village. Calling the Twelve to him, he sent them out two by two and gave them authority over evil spirits" (Mark 6:6–7). In regard to evil spirits, I will talk about this in another chapter.

Jesus Leads the Way

There is no doubt that Jesus had a specific goal in mind, and that was to make disciples. It was clear from the father what He had to do. His first stop was at the Jordan River. He had to be baptized in order to sanction His discipleship focus and purpose. After his baptism, (Matthew 3:16) he was now stronger to face his temptation. He knew what had to be done. He knew what it took in order to complete the task. Jesus was determined not to allow the cunningness of Satan especially during His temptation (Matthew 4: 1–11) to get in His way. He had a long journey ahead of Him, but He was committed for the task from baptism to crucifixion. Jesus was focused on preparing His disciples to continue His work before His ascension on the Mount of Olives.

The real test of His disciples came after He left them. All they had was what Jesus left with them. He left them the Holy Spirit (John 16:7) to guide them and comfort them in all that they had to do. Jesus went from seeking them to sending them. When He made His ascension back to the Father, (Mark 16:19; Luke 24:50–51) he left the church in good hands.

Compassion and Care In order for the church to be the image of Jesus Christ, she must have the spirit *of* compassion for everyone. Compassion can't just be shown to a select group of people, but everyone in the church and the community. If the church seriously desires to make it as a New Testament Church, she must have compassion and care. Therefore, the leadership *of* the church must advocate the following principles:

1. The Plain Truth Every disciple of Christ is in good hands. There is no wavering *of* any kind regarding what is the real meaning *of* this work *of* ministry The only way to follow Jesus correctly is to accept reality without complaining. The truth is that Jesus set things in order. And what He has set in order cannot be changed or altered. What is needed today is the truth. The truth shall set one free.

2. Committed to the Task The state of a person who is dedicated is shown through his or her commitment. The church helps others understand discipleship and what has to happen. The truth must be known to people from all walks of life. This is where commitment challenges the church to keep on track at all times. There must not be any wavering or wandering, hesitation or reservation.

3. Simplicity The church must stress both theory and practice. Theory here means to explain the Word of God with both spirit and substance. Therefore, the church must present the Bible in a clear and practical manner in order that all people can understand and apply it in their lives.

When we follow in the footsteps of Jesus, we will receive great blessings of happiness and live in obedience to the command of Christ. Without following in the footsteps of Jesus, there is no way that the church can survive and grow into maturity. Jesus promotes growing healthy. The above suggested principles pave the way for churches to keep the real focus on leading others to a richer and more fulfilled life. Every disciple must be courageous regarding the Master's plan of discipleship.

STUDY REVIEW GUIDE: STRONG FOUNDATION

Biblical Truth

The church must continue in the footsteps of Jesus.

Key Word

AUTHORITY: The Greek word for authority is *exousia*, "which means, the power of one's will and command is to be obeyed by others." (In this case it is Jesus)

> *Memory Verses*
>
> Matthew 28:18–20

Point of Emphasis

Discipling others can't be done without interaction. Jesus really interacted with His disciples. He desired that they would learn.

Theological Reflection

Your theological views and reflection from this study.

Personal Application

Your thoughts on how this study has impacted you.

Study Questions

1. Discuss what it means to help others grow into healthy disciples.

2. What is your understanding of discipleship?

3. How does your church understand discipleship?

4. How does the biblical truth relate to your ministry?

5. How much do you think your church cares about discipleship?

A Revolutionary Foundation

Implementing the Missionary Mandate

> "One day Jesus called together his twelve apostles and gave them power and authority to cast out demons and to heal all diseases." (Luke 9:1)

Knowing the meaning of how to implement is an added asset for the church today.

One of the primary responsibilities of the church is to know what to focus on. When one is focused, one can implement effectively. There are many distractions which cause the church to be unfocused. No matter the difficulty, staying focused is crucial. We shall emphasize biblical models that churches can model which will constitute a foundation utilizing missionary principles for discipleship ministry. My argument in this chapter is, in order to be an authentic disciple, one must do missionary work. One must be willing to go beyond the normal missionary duty, which includes evangelism. Evangelism is an integral part of the Missionary Mandate. People must work together and build relationships. This is a key factor in implementing the Missionary Mandate. "What a church proclaims through the interpersonal relationships of its members has great influence on the church's reputation in the community from which it draws new members."[10]

We shall now turn our focus on the models which will validate the church's ministry which will lead to healthy disciples. As the main model for the church, Jesus is the expert on training. His disciples were focused when given their kingdom assignment on earth. This assignment was most important. It was an assignment designed to change individuals. All other assignments hinge on the above verse. As said earlier every believer is really a missionary. Missionaries are not only confined to a small group of people in the church. So therefore, every church has to step up to the missionary call and prepare individuals for the field. In the Greek, the word for call in this passage is *sungkaelo,* meaning "to call together." *Sung* means together and *kaelo* means to call. The text serves as its own exposition when it says, "Then He called His twelve together..."(Luke 9:1). Regardless of what Jesus had to face, and the oppositions which challenged Him, He still called His disciples together. In order for Jesus to chart the course, being together showed that everyone was on one accord. He commissioned them for a special journey. He did not give them a long dissertation on this assignment. He was concise and to the point.

The church must be extremely committed to the ministry of discipleship through the imparting of God's Word.

Part 1: The Foundation Factor

Before the church can impart God's Word, disciples must be called together and given instruction. They must clearly know what their specific mission is. The truth must not only be explained, but it must also be implemented. Jesus empowered His disciples to go forward. In order for the church to break forth new disciples and train them for ministry, there must be an on-going training program for spiritual development. This means that churches should have a context for doing ministry.

Therefore, the ministry of discipleship should emphasize being close together, i.e. ministering in small groups and forming small circles. To be candid, the church is hurting because some people do not study enough. I am reminded of a vehicle that has working parts, spark plugs, a battery and all the necessary working parts to make the automobile run, to discover that the gas is not getting to the fuel injection or the older cars the carburetor. If the fuel does not get to these channels, then the car will not run, all it does is turn over. Disciples are like carburetors and fuel injectors; they channel God's Word to others and aid them in operating to their full capacity for Jesus. The church does not need clogged up carburetors and fuel injectors that are impeding the flow of spiritual fuel as sharing the Word.

There must be a suitable place for teaching, nurturing and training. There is a need for the church to do effective discipleship in a viable working environment. A positive atmosphere is a must for developing disciples. In *The Master's Plan for Discipleship,* authors Arn & Arn call the huddle a "Holy Huddle."[11] We need players on the team. Twelve players need to come together and get the discipleship play together and help move the church in a positive direction. Disciples need encouragement and motivation. Disciples need time to be alone with Christ.

When it comes to the imparting God's Word, it is not left solely to the preacher. Every individual in the Body of Christ is responsible for ministering to others. There is no excuse for the church to not be able to teach God's Word with authority. Jesus gave the authority because He is the authority. Every church would be far better off when every individual take seriously the road to disciple-making a Christ enterprise. The church really must have the cooperation from parishioners who know the value of commitment. That is why the Bible says, "But you will receive power when the Holy Spirit comes on you; and you will be my witnesses in Jerusalem, and in all Judea and Samaria, and to the ends of the earth" (Acts 1:8). The church has to have power to do the Kingdom's work.

When one is committed then one will share the gospel in the hearts and minds of many that may not know Him. Just as Jesus gave His disciples power over all demons, and to cure diseases, He still is in the demon demolition business. His focus is to eradicate all evil and cure all diseases. Christ has given the church the formula in the form of power; authority and the healing touch. The key to get rid of demons and sickness is through preaching and teaching. Crowds followed Him (Mark 5:21–43, Matthew 13:1–3). Crowds could not and would not accept anything but to witness Jesus at work restoring broken fellowships, renewing old fellowships and making new acquaintances. The church must work together regarding making credible disciples.

PART 1: THE FOUNDATION FACTOR

Jesus' Model for the Church's Mission

The ministry of discipleship is a specific mission. It requires that individuals be totally committed. To be committed means going beyond the normal daily routine of ministry. Jesus was not territorial to one or two areas. He ministered to the felt needs of the people. Commitment requires blood sweat and tears. There will be many sleepless nights. The only way that churches and individuals can be blessed and have the opportunity to grow, is to be keep the faith. Jesus ministered in the surrounding areas of Galilee, the hills and of Judea, and even as far as Caeseara Philippi. He prepared His disciples for a broader ministry than what they expected. It is important for the church to create a mission statement and a mission purpose.

The ministry of discipleship should be reflected in the church's mission statement. The mission statement states the intent and desire of the congregation. The purpose tells why it is done.

It is my belief that the church is obligated to develop and prepare individuals to be wise, witness, and win others for the sake of the kingdom of God (Acts 8:4). This means that the church must be ready to step out on faith and tread deeper waters. Therefore, I believe that every church must be sensitive to the needs of struggling, undeveloped and undernourished disciples. They are underdeveloped and undernourished in regards to their own growth as responsible disciples.

I am not saying that all disciples fit this description, however, these disciples are not capable of discipling others and winning them. Going beyond traditional territory requires breaking through cultural and ethnic barriers. I am not suggesting that one pressure or push their way to another ethnic group, but to merely use a positive approach and inform people that the church is open to serving all people regardless of their tradition. Jesus laid the foundation for reaching others through His passion and in spreading the gospel. The Apostle Paul builds on the foundation of Christ. Paul reminded the Corinthian Church the importance of building on the right foundation (I Corinthians 3:10–11).

The church in the twenty-first century must proclaim the gospel to all. It will be a weak church to try and make the gospel headquarters at their church for their own people. This is to say that we are to meet and nourish people where they are, local and global. Many parishioners in many churches across the United States prayerfully desire to be loyal to God, but are not fully living up to being what one claims to be. Mission work places great responsibility on the church. It is the core of the existence. Its strategy must be biblically based and theologically sound. People must be convinced that the pulse of the church is divinely connected and that there is an ongoing relationship among the people of God.

Pauline Model for a Mission Defined

As it was previously said, Jesus paved the way for unlocking the door of opportunity to minister across culture. No church should wait around until there is a perfect time to meet strangers, it just will not happen. Everyday we are on a mission for God. The problem is that we must identify with the mission for the Glory of God. Paul Beals, a noted scholar has done extensive work on missions, states the following:

Talk about being culture-bound! And Paul knew what he

believed, too! But meeting Jesus on the Damascus Road made all the difference (Acts 9:1–19). Paul believed Christ's claims, was born again by the Spirit, and now walked in the newness of life" (Romans 6:4, KJV). He viewed all religious and cultural heritage as "rubbish, that I may gain Christ and be found in him…(Philippians 3: 8–9). God turned Paul about-face from persecuting churches to planting churches. All this happened in the space of twelve to fifteen years.[12]

Paul had a passion for mission. He was focused on bringing cultures together for the common good of his day. In doing this, the gospel was central to his ministry. Paul also placed much emphasis on the cross of Christ and His resurrection. He was more concerned about Christ in their life than culture. "Paul or any other Apostle did not see culture and scripture on the same plane. When faith in Christ produces a new faith the lifestyle of that person changes. A new value system takes over. A Christ-centered life results in cultural changes as well as spiritual."[13] Paul clearly advocates that our commitment should be on Christ.

When a person bids Christ, there is change, and new waters are charted. Paul was in the face of cultural diversity with many groups. The reason that he was so successful in reaching different cultures is because he was busy planting churches. Paul was not in any way bashful, but was straight forward. He had a mission to accomplish. This mission was evident in his appeal to King Agrippa, in which he was almost successful (Acts 26: 26–29). He was preparing himself to sail to Italy to proclaim the gospel (Acts 27:1–8).

Regardless of oppositions, Paul's charge was to preach the gospel, nothing different. This opposition came from the Jews who witnessed the preaching of the gospel (Acts 13:44–45). Paul and Barnabas were missionary partners. They were much stronger together. This teamwork got attention from the resistant Jews. Paul is a good model for the 21st Century church because of his widespread appeal to convert the unsaved.

Models in God's Church

Key Approaches for Growing Disciples

1. Prospecting for Potential Disciples Every church and every disciple should desire to want to see the church grow. Therefore, the church should develop a prospecting plan inclusive of both inside and outside the church. In every congregation there lies a seedbed of potential disciples. They are like ripe grapes waiting to be picked. The problem is that they are overlooked, or sometimes are assumed credible and faithful disciples.

The process of prospecting requires advanced training. This training means that everyone who goes beyond the traditional territory requires breaking through cultural and ethnic prospects. The church must know what to say and do. Let me give a more graphic example: Many years ago I was employed as an insurance agent for one of the leading insurance companies in the south. The company required that every agent prospected daily and weekly for new clients. Their feeling was based on statistics, that people was under insured. The provided brochures briefly explaining the basic coverage of each plan of insurance. In other words, they had a plan, which would be suitable for each individual or family.

I was one of their top sellers for many years. I was successful in using two methods for effective prospecting. The first method was cold canvassing. Cold canvassing is when you meet people any place and give them a brochure. It is meeting strangers. In cold canvassing, one must sell themselves and approach people with a conviction. The second method was referrals. Someone would always tell his or her friends of the product/s that were available. This means that referrals kept coming. There were agents who used the telephone as one of their methods. I only used the telephone in rare cases.

Just as insurance companies used the above methods, cold canvassing, referrals and telephone, the church can adopt and utilize the same. Churches should train individuals to be able to meet people. It takes courage to cold canvass. Also be prepared to accept the following responses: I am not interested, there are too many hypocrites in the church, the preacher is only after money, people don't care, and I don't have the right clothes. In some cases, some of these may be true; believers must not become discouraged or disappointed with these reasons.

Another method for prospecting for new disciples is to send letters. Sending letters to new residents and visitors thanking them for attending and that they are welcome to the church. Give them some literature about the church and pastor. This method gives them time to think and reflect about the church and the leadership. Regardless of the method or methods used, the church must know how to present the Word of God, and when the time comes, be prepared to share the plan of salvation.

2. Sharing the Plan of Salvation Sharing the plan of salvation is the key action plan. If there is no sharing of the plan, there is no opportunity for salvation. The evangelical church needs to initiate its method for what I call "Know and Show." Churches must know the plan and show the plan. Jesus prepared His disciples to go out and share the plan of salvation with the world. Before the plan of salvation can be shared, it is a good idea to give a brief introduction of self and the church you represent.

In presenting the plan of salvation, one must talk about the grace of God and tell others it is free; it is unearned, unmerited and undeserving. There is nothing that we can do to achieve it. In showing the plan, tell them that "For the wages of sin is death, but the gift of God is eternal life in Christ Jesus our Lord" (Romans 6:23). In this passage, gift comes from the Greek word, Charisma which means a gift of grace involving God as the donor. It is necessary to mention man as a sinner, "but all have sinned and come short of the glory of God" (Romans 3:23). In regards to salvation, we are saved by the grace of God. Ephesians 2:8, 9 states that "For it is by grace you have been saved, through faith—and this not from yourselves, it is the gift of God—not by works, so that no one can boast." The evangelical church, the church that is striving to master discipleship must present Jesus as the Savior. Jesus must be presented because it was because of His blood that washed our sins away.

Many scholars and theologians characterize the plan of salvation as the Roman Road to salvation, which is different from the Gospels. According to the Roman Road to salvation, the first step in being saved is confession. Paul states, "That if you confess with your mouth the Lord Jesus and believe in your heart that God has raised Him from the dead, you will be saved"(Romans 10:9). The word confess in the above passage comes form the Greek verb Homologeo, meaning to be honest and admitting guilt. This is quite different from the emphasis of John the Baptist and Jesus who preached repentance. Repentance comes from the Greek word Metanoia, which means a change of mind or a turning around of a troubled and rebellious life in responding to God's proposal for a new life. What is the difference or similarity? There is a fundamental difference between confession and repentance. The fundamental difference is that confession is first and repentance is second. One cannot change his or her mind until the facts of the gospel has been made available.

3. Promoting Spiritual Renewal Every Christian must desire to live an anointed life. Every church should be bursting with excitement regarding discipleship. People should want renewal. Church leaders should pray for renewal. This passion for having the desire for growing disciples will set new spiritual horizons for ministry. This desire to see this ministry strive is a result of an honest assessment of church health and church growth. These indicators come from years of pastoring and teaching both in the church and seminaries have added to this invaluable list. Here are some common indicators for detecting the uprising potency of a lack of church renewal. These are by no means an exhaustive list for identifying a lack of church renewal.

- A lack of disciple-making is an indication of a lack of church renewal.
- A lack of prayer is an indication of a lack of renewal.

- A lack of the studying of the Word is an indication of a lack of renewal.

- A lack of giving is an indication of a lack or renewal.

- Poor fellowship is an indication of a lack of renewal.

- Low church attendance and participation are an indication of a lack of renewal.

- A poor appreciation for evangelism is an indication for as lack of renewal

- Increased immorality is an indication of a lack of renewal.

- An inadequate training program is an indication of a lack of renewal.

- A lack of advocating missions is an indication of a lack of renewal.

The church must realize that there is a need for church renewal. Therefore, leaders must want renewal. Without renewal, disciple-making has neither strength nor strategy for developing others. Some people constantly reject basic biblical principles. This is because they have balloon attitudes, which are woven into their own cognitive ignorance. In other words, they feel that there is no or little need for renewal. There is no satisfaction when one knows that he or she needs spiritual food. Jesus said "those who hunger and thirst after righteousness shall be filled" (Matthew 6:4). A deep hunger for the Word of God makes one more aware of what God can and will do. When people hunger, they hunger for discipleship.

When one opens up and pours his or her soul out to God is a sure sign of righteousness. It is guaranteed that one will be filled. A deep hunger for the Word of God is a sign of spiritual maturity and spiritual growth. Being hungry and getting food is one thing. We have food from Genesis to Revelation. Parishioners can receive food anytime.

The church must have a divine purpose in mind while making sure that the Word gets to the intended receiver. What makes people desire to be filled with the Word? The answer is that they have a relationship with God. They have been saved. I will talk more about salvation later. Now I want to focus on people having an appreciation for the Word.

It is not the role of the church to pressure people to seek spiritual renewal, but to encourage them. To encourage people to become serious students of God's Word is most beneficial and urgent for the ministry of discipleship. Most people need some encouragement in order to discipline themselves for a dedicated spiritual life. People need time for reflection and meditation. They need to reflect on their own personal spiritual growth. They need to seriously meditate on becoming what God would have them to do. In order to do this, there are three key principles that the discipling church must advocate: (1) Identifying potential disciples (2) Nurturing potential disciples through small groups (3) Motivating and encouraging present disciples.

4. Identifying Potential Disciples Before a church can provide teaching, preaching and developing of disciples, the primary responsibility is to first identify potential disciples. Because of the many distractions and attractions of churches today, it is not that easy. Identifying potential disciples requires much prayer and patience. The purpose of identifying potential disciples is for adequate preparation of reaching the world. Jesus identified specific men to be His disciples. "The ministry of Jesus Christ began with the call of Peter and Andrew, and James and John to be disciples; and it closed with the commission given to those whom He called His disciples to go into all the world to make disciples of all nations."[14] The reason for this identification was to get their commitment and cooperation to win the world. It is clear in everything that the church does; it must be based on the model and criteria that Jesus designed. Jesus identified or rather called Peter, Andrew, James and John to work with Him. Unlike what Jesus did, the church can only identify individuals to be leaders in the ministry of discipleship to help reach the world.

There are perhaps numerous ways of identifying potential disciples. One way to identify them is through their Christian walk. This means that they are eager to become nurtured through teaching and training. Their appetite for spiritual growth has increased. Another way to identify them is through their faith commitment, which will be discussed later in this work.

In every business, major employers are spending millions of dollars advertising for skillful and credible workers. In order for the business to make progress, there must be accountability in rising to meet new standards for effectiveness. Many employers make their selection of skillful workers through the method of evaluation. They train from within in many cases. The same holds true for churches. Any church that is not engaged in the business of identifying disciples is making poor progress and not focusing on the missionary mandate.

No focus, no disciples, no focus, no fruit. The leadership of the pastor must set the stage and chart the course. Paul makes it clear in Ephesians 4:11–12 that pastors are responsible for preparing disciples for the work of ministry. The goal of the church should be to get at the business of identifying disciples.

5. Developing Potential Disciples through Small Groups
There is no way for churches to develop and nurture the masses without realizing the need to start with small groups. Small group ministry is the epitome of managing the masses. The masses grow because of small groups. Jesus said, "For where two or three come together in my name, there am I with them" (Matthew 18:20). This passage sheds light on the fact that Jesus will honor our sincerity, faithfulness and prayer for each other in unity. Therefore, we must nurture each other through caring and loving. Just as it is significant to grow churches through small groups, if the purpose, focus and motive are clear, small churches can develop, depending who is leading the small groups.

However, no matter how small or large the church, the reality is that there is going to be some allegiance to each other in the group. This is because trust and a sense of community are developed in small groups. "Creating a sense of participation and ownership in people is the key to successfully using small groups in any church."[15] The small group ministry is designed to strengthen the church, rather than to stifle it. It is to develop it and not divide it. Its purpose should be to multiply and make disciples. I will discuss the process of multiplication in detail later in another chapter.

There is a major advantage in developing the small group

ministry. Small group ministry challenges the church to widen its potential in seeking prepared leaders to be coordinators and facilitators for this needed ministry. Those churches desiring church growth must intimately institute the cell group ministry. Cell group ministry focuses on building an intimate relationship with God through the group. The intention is to build a cell church. Joel Comiskey defines a cell church, he says, in everyday terminology; it's simply a church that has placed evangelistic small groups at the core of its ministry. Cell ministry is not another program; it's the very heart of the church."[16] Small group ministry keeps the church on track in being responsible for discipleship, stewardship, evangelism and missions. Any church will grow by leaps and bounds through small groups. There are many churches, new and old using the cell group approach. Small group ministry is the motive and mission of the new millennium. The only problem is that in some churches, groups will create churches within the church. Therefore, the purpose must be reiterated more than once by the pastor and the Director of Christian education.

6. Motivating and Encouraging Disciples **After Jesus had** established His disciples, He never took for granted that they needed continued motivation and encouragement. Make no mistake about it; Jesus spent time with His disciples. Many times believers will become discouraged concerning what will take place tomorrow. When too much worry takes place, it causes one to lose his or her focus on discipleship. Jesus knew that His disciples would have problems and disappointments. It is clear that the Master gave His disciples a lesson on how to deal with their anxiety (Matthew 6:25–34).

In order to eliminate frustration with His disciples, He specifically connects His earthly ministry to the work of the Holy Spirit in His absence (John 16:7–15). With this in mind, John establishes the continuity of His ministry as being represented by the Holy Spirit. This is another way that the Master will be with His people. Jesus wanted His disciples to experience the ministry of the Holy Spirit. The Holy Spirit was to give them some great sense of hope and encouragement. The Holy Spirit convicts the world of sin and righteousness. True believers will definitely have to minister to individuals in the presence of sin. Having to face sin and knowing what to do will determine one's commitment.

Mastering the Mandate: A Church focused Strategy

It was stated earlier that Jesus chose a select group of disciples to train as leaders. It must be made clear that the entire church is responsible for the advocacy of the ministry of discipleship. The way in which the church can assure that new converts understands the focus of reaching others is that they develop a sense of responsibility. Once one knows responsibility, then one is ready to become an integral part of the ministry. A focused strategy for leading others to mastering the mandate is a significant objective of the church. This strategy initiates and enables the church to develop major steps in the strategizing process. Every church should have biblical and theological standards for becoming skilled disciples.

Churches must set their priority to become masters of the mandate that Christ has directed through His teachings. The simple way to master the mandate is to follow the pattern set forth by the Master of discipleship training. A good example is found in the words of Jesus, "In the same way, let your light shine before men, that they may see your good deeds and praise your Father in heaven" (Matthew 5:13). There is no option regarding mastering the mandate. Every church must set out to make this a priority.

Disciples of Christ cannot effectively master the mandate of making disciples with dim and dull lights. It is important to be able to see. The Bible says, "But you are a chosen people, a royal priesthood, a holy nation, a people belonging to God, that you may declare the praises of him who called you out of darkness into his wonderful light" (I Pet 2:9). The eyes of the world are watching the church. This means that in reality, the world looks to the church for spiritual guidance. In order to guide others, there must be illumination, illumination of mind, thought and character. Whatever the church does, please continue to please God while serving and meeting the needs of the community. I would like to suggest three factors for effectuating the church focused strategy for leadership development.

Association

Association is the key for the beginning of a new experience in disciple-making. If there is no association, there is no assimilation for the local church. A church with an association complex, will certainty draw the new parishioners and make them welcome. Many churches need to pride themselves in association. I have experienced people who think that they can accomplish the disciple-making ministry by themselves. The task of disciple-making is too big for one person to do it all. This means that many sit back and watch how others do it, and they end up criticizing and complaining about what is happening. Although in many churches, there are those who are left alone to accomplish this task without assistance from others. Jesus associated with His disciples and developed a close and intimate relationship with each of them. Association was the nucleus for their training. Just as Jesus did, we too have to love people, and love them with passion.

Imitation

The use of the word imitation in our culture has meant to be a copycat. We are told it is better to be original and not be a clone of someone else. Although, everyone should have a role model or a mentor who can help shape their lives and encourage them. It has been said that it is impossible to be you and imitate someone else. Disciple-making denotes clearly that there is a need to pattern the very moves and structure of Jesus. Therefore, imitation means that the church has to do exactly what Jesus says and does.

If the church is going to be effective in growing disciples, following Jesus and developing a theology of discipleship is essential for our faith. Peter imitated Jesus when he walked on the water. The minute he took his eyes off of Jesus, he began to sink on the Sea of Galilee. "This means that the church must strive to train leaders who are willing to imitate Christ and never take their eyes off of Him. To imitate Christ means to walk in His footsteps and provide ministry to fallen humanity. Imitate means to inform and instruct others in biblical and theological foundations for building a viable discipleship program in the church. After imitation, comes implementation.

Implementation

Now this factor is to stress the nuts and bolts of mastering the mandate. Saying one thing and doing another are not in juxtaposition with each other. Jesus demonstrated to His disciples how to implement the principles in which He taught. Implementation reveals the hidden work of the church, bringing it to the forefront. It is the evidence of hard work, sweat and tears of practicing ministry. If the church can't make disciples, then the church needs to evaluate its approach and methods on how to develop disciples.

It is very important to be able to put things in action and make them happen. Making things happen is a true sign of implementing principles. More and more churches need to place emphasis on implementation. Regardless of how we associate or imitate, the real need is the strategy of how things are done. Implementation requires a stated objective of the church's overall ministry. Here are some suggestions for implementing the ministry of discipleship:

Develop a discipleship team made of lay leaders to help train new disciples. This team keeps individuals informed with information regarding discipleship. These individuals will be responsible for guiding and helping implementing the strategies and approaches for effective ministry.

There must be networking with other churches and ministries through sharing information. This networking is to bring about a change in leading people and helping them in their faith. Networking keeps the church healthy and alive in reaching its potential. Leaders and groups in the church must work with each other to create a better working environment. Competition should never be the center of focus among groups or churches, but there should be constant correspondence. Each group should have a team leader and that person should be responsible for helping new workers in the group to commit themselves to the overall ministry of the group. The point is that everyone has a specific role or task to accomplish. This will eliminate confusion because the church is on a mission and that we need everyone to help accomplish this mission.

While the church is implementing the ministry of mission, it is important to be aware of the following: When the church sends out individuals, they must be prepared for the booby traps in mine fields. Satan planted mines in the field a long time ago. When God sends us on a mission, He sends us with a message to validate the authenticity of the mission. The church must not forget that the mission of the church belongs to God exclusively.

I will share a personal story when I was serving in the U.S. Armed forces. I was serving overseas in Korea in 1967. We were on a maneuver one morning. Our staff Sergeant led us through a minefield where mines were used during the Korean War. We were told to walk five meters behind each solider and three meters from the left side of the path. I had the instructions precise. Our staff sergeant was walking off course, and I warned him, but he told me he was alright. Immediately after that, he stepped onto a mine. I shared that story because it is precisely what the church will encounter on a daily basis. Traps are set and we must know which way to walk and how far.

Application

The church must make sure that each individual who plans to share the gospel with others that they are fully aware of the process of application. Application is putting into practice step by step of what one has learned. Jesus taught his disciples to practice what was real. They had to deal with hands on issues and daily concerns. It does not matter what and how impressive the discipleship plan is, if the plan can't meet the needs of the people, they will go elsewhere. People want transformation, purpose and direction. They must see clearly what you are doing, and where you are going. This is the stage where the church can't afford to become lackadaisical and content.

In every phase of the ministry of the church, application is a key component for the survival of the ministry. Ministry is not authentic until the ministry is applied. Unlike association, imitation and implementation, application recaps all of the above in a unique way. This is because application has its own strategy in the sense that it challenges the church to take a closer look at its methodology for doing ministry. If what is taught is not shared in a practical and positive manner, ministry will not be effective.

I have discovered that sermons on discipleship as well as others should apply truths that are well thought out. Preaching must meet people where they are and provide hope for where their needs are. With a captivating audience, the Word of God reaches the hearts of the listeners and leaves a compelling challenge to take what has been heard and run to the streets sharing the message of salvation. Our relationship with God is grounded in our faith. Fellowship affirms in others that they matter. I believe that this cycle is needed in order to maximize God's mission as true followers of Christ. *(See Diagram 3)*

Diagram 3

Missionary Support Cycle

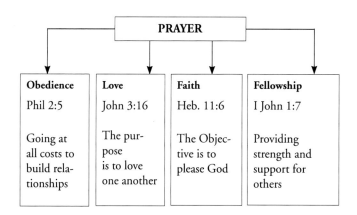

STUDY REVIEW GUIDE: A REVOLUTIONARY FOUNDATION

Biblical Truth

Every believer is a missionary.

Key Word

WITNESS: The Greek word for witness is *martus* which means "one who bears witness and can share what he or she has seen or heard"

Memory Verse

Acts 1:8

Point of Emphasis

It is important to have a deep theological view on mission.

Theological Reflection

Your theological views and reflection from this study.

Personal Application

Your thoughts on how this study has impacted you.

Study Questions

1. Why is it necessary for the church to have a theological view of mission?

2. Why is a strong faith needed to call the church to total commitment?

3. Why are so many churches lax when it comes to doing mission?

4. How does the biblical truth relate to your ministry?

5. Why is a church focused strategy for mission work is important?

PART 2

THE HARVEST FACTOR

This section is a critical section in this book. It is serious because if the church is not concerned about the harvest, then the meaning and significance of kingdom building must be revisited. The harvest includes people from all walks of life. People are doing different things, but one thing they have in common is that they need attention. There is an attention deficit in many churches regarding discipleship. This does not mean that no one is doing discipleship in churches. I am saying there needs to be more. The premise of this section is to motivate churches to go to the harvest and do it immediately! I heard a preacher who preached a sermon in Florida, and his title was: "The Church needs to go to Hell." The emphasis of the message was that the community is like hell, and the church has been commissioned to rectify human condition and reclaim the ministry of discipleship. Churches must be willing to invest in the harvest. This means that churches have to change their course of direction and really be about the business of the kingdom. There is enough work for every church and individuals. If churches do not go to the harvest, then the church will become the harvest and others will have to minister to the church.

4

Responding to the Harvest

What the Church should Do

> He said to his disciples, "The harvest is so great, but the workers are so few. So pray to the Lord who is in charge of the harvest; ask him to send out more workers for his fields." (Matthew 9:37–38, NLT)

Working the harvest is a sign of a true disciple. As a believer, you are responsible to respond to a ripe harvest. This is part of the missionary responsibility. The harvest that I am referring to is a day-to-day harvest of ministering to people. It is center stage, and it is ripe and overflowing with needs that need to be attended to. The harvest is the community of the unsaved. It is when and where people are hurt and burdened.

God's church is exposed to a matrix of contacts and experiences to describe a ripe harvest. The harvest is people who have no hope, they are searching to be transformed, and receive conformation that the church cares. The harvest is those who have lost respect for the church and they need to be reclaimed. The harvest is really a life that one feels he or she is living in pure hell. Therefore the church needs to go there to deliver them from pain and suffering. They need to be saved from sin.

The first thing that the church should do is pray. We need to pray that Jesus will send more to work the harvest. Jesus knew what he would do regarding those who will come and respond to a ripe harvest, but he wanted to encourage his disciples to pray. The harvest is full, but there are many vacancies to be filled for the harvest. Working in the harvest requires one to be fruitful. Jesus really taught his disciples a lesson on the meaning of fruit. "I am the vine; you are the branches. If a man remains in me and I in him, he will bear much fruit; apart from me you can do nothing. If anyone does not remain in me, he is like a branch that is thrown away and withers; such branches are picked up, thrown into the fire and burned. If you remain in me and my words remain in you, ask whatever you wish, and it will be given you. This is to my Father's glory, that you bear much fruit, showing yourselves to be my disciples" (John 15:5–8). Responding to the needs of people can and will be rewarding. It can be rewarding because this is God's will.

People all around you are waiting to hear the gospel message because "this harvest will exceed every precious outpouring of the Spirit in one profound way-Jesus will be preached as Lord and not just Savior. During this harvest the gospel will change from come and be saved, to "Bow the knee, He is the King!¹⁷" The harvest was ripe during Pentecost when Peter preached and three thousand souls were saved. The Bible says, "On that day about three thousand believed his message and were baptized" (Acts 2:41, CEV). The harvest has never been any riper than now. Quiet as it is kept, people from almost all cultures, backgrounds, ethnicities, and religions are seeking new answers to their spiritual questions. They are searching for answers regarding eternity now. There is no time for procrastination. There is never a better time than now to work the harvest. Jesus said, "Do you not say, 'Four months more and then the harvest'? I tell you, open your eyes and look at the fields! They are ripe for harvest" (John 4:35). People can be riding on a train, bus, sailing on a ship, flying in a plane, sitting in a barbershop, hair salon, etc., or holding a conversation with someone concerning salvation. People ears are wide open. Watch their eyes, and one can tell. If you don't lead them to Christ, eventually someone else will, and you would have lost the blessing of sharing Christ.

Therefore, since you are part of the church, then the task of the church should as much as possible utilize every believer in the local church to work the harvest and provide answers to these important questions. In actuality, responding to a ripe harvest is really a servant-hood task because the church has been commissioned for this work. The harvest is ready, but the question is are we ready for the harvest?

We are not to worry about who is in the harvest, that's God's concern. The harvest is a time of reaping and sowing. Jesus said, responding to a ripe harvest is true discipleship in action. Therefore, Jesus, "When He saw the crowds, He had compassion for them, because they were harassed and helpless, like sheep without a shepherd" (Matthew 9:36). You have to act like you want to work the harvest. Everyone living will get the opportunity to hear the gospel. This is really an evangelism explosion. It is an explosion based on the response from people from all walks of life. Jesus also said, "The harvest is the end of time" (Matthew 13:39, CEV). Harvest here means now and the close of the age in which we live. This means that the name of Jesus will be heard from all walks of life.

Jesus is preparing for the harvest. He is expecting many to accept Him as their personal Savior. There has been a misconception in church that working the harvest is solely left up to the pastor. The people of God are responsible for working the harvest, because in order to work the harvest, it takes duplicating ourselves in others. The responsibility of the pastor is to lead and do the equipping, while the people do the evangelizing. The people of God are considered the laity. The word laity comes from the Greek word, Laos, meaning the people of God. Each person is ordained by God to carry out the purpose and function of the ministry. The work of the church is not solely left up to the pastor but a shared ministry between the people of God.

People get caught up in the context of churchship rather than discipleship. Churchship simply means doing every thing other than growing disciples. It is at the wishes of the local congregation. One can get tired doing church work, and never do the work of the church. Church work is working on committees with no purpose, attending to your own agenda, or other insignificant tasks.

The work of the church is discipleship, evangelism, and missions. Churchship is my terminology for describing what many do in the church. Sometimes what people do in the church is not necessary for the benefit of the Kingdom. What is done in the church has to have a divine purpose only to satisfy God. Developing and duplicating disciples for the harvest requires total commitment and dedication. Commitment and dedication are rooted in the process of duplication. Discipleship duplication is adding to the Body of Christ.

The Process of Discipleship Duplication

In order for any individual or group to help others to grow, duplication is a needed process. Reaching the harvest requires duplicating new believers to help accomplish the goal of outreach. The objective is that each one, reach one. Duplication is the result of hard work, patience and dedication. The following formula is a suggested formula for growing dedicated disciples in today's church.

$$\frac{HW + CC}{NW} = PR$$

The formula is *hard work plus clear communication* divided by needed workers *will equal positive results.* Workers are always needed in the church. Every believer should be responsible. Duplication is really doing ministry one on one. It is evangelism hands on.

The Great Commission is really the ministry of duplication. As a disciple, you are responsible for leading others to Christ. You can't be saved and sit, because you are sanctified for service. You are either "sitting on the premises or standing on the promises." You are blessed when you are standing on the promises. You are stagnant when you are sitting on the premises. Sitting on the premises mean that some just waste time and do not value their salvation and have no desire to encourage others to be saved. Thank God that the entire church is not sitting. You must determine your *service status* in the Body of Christ. It is important to keep the Great Commission in focus for effective ministry. Every church and every believer must have a clear stated plan for developing disciples. A clear focus is an asset for a healthy ministry.

A Working Methodology

Methodology deals with the way in which people do what they do. When there is no method, things will not move smoothly. A method gives direction as to how things will be done. When people are in small groups, they are expecting direction and not confusion. One of the worst things that can happen to a church is a derailment for a lack of clarity on the part of leaders. The goal of any church is to make sure that everyone understands. This means that the purpose statement must be clear. Clear directions and instructions will eliminate confusion. A working methodology will help the church to grow positively.

The Need for Motivation

Every church experiences a lack of motivation. There is sometimes a high and a low. It is either motivation or intimidation. A lack of motivation really makes a statement: "we just don't have what it takes to do ministry." The Holy Spirit has to ignite Holy Fire in the hearts and minds of both pastor and people. One can work the harvest when the Holy Spirit is leading.

Many churches would do better if they would stop making excuses for not fulfilling the Great Commission of Christ. We should be witnessing instead of whining. When I use the term whining, I am not castigating churches in a negative sense, but I feel that there is a need to encourage other churches to quit complaining about what can't be done. The church in the twenty-first century has to adopt newer ideas and methods to effectively work the harvest. These newer methods will increase motivation and encourage parishioners to do better. In addition to these methods, there are two major components for encouraging believers to share the gospel.

COMPONENT ONE

Relational Evangelism

Discipleship training is an important step in the life of the church as well as the individual. Every believer is an evangelist. The first step in developing and training disciples is to begin with evangelism and the second is follow-up. Evangelism is the key focus of the Great Commission. It is the key focus because it opens the door for discipleship. Training is the necessary element to keep people ready for the harvest. It is important for each disciple to have adequate training. Without proper training, churches will suffer and there will be a decline in spiritual growth. Churches must set a criterion for those who are leaders and they should be trained to become genuine disciples.

The training process of discipleship is an ongoing process.

After evangelism has been established, follow-up is necessary. New disciples need nourishment and care as an ongoing mentorship. The plan of salvation should be taught to them, and as they develop, they can focus on helping others to do likewise. These new disciples cannot be left alone; they need guidance because they are eager. Peter shares this remarkable verse concerning discipleship growth, "Like newborn babies, crave pure spiritual milk, so that by it you may grow up in your salvation" (I Peter 2:2). Another follow-up approach for training disciples is to encourage them to have their personal devotional time with God. Devotional time is receiving spiritual strength.

The new disciple in training must be taught basic Christian doctrine. New members' orientation should be made available. Classes should be clear, simple and practical. It is not good to overwhelm the new disciple with too much information at one time. They must be spoon fed at first until they discover their developmental process. Terms such as righteousness, justification, regeneration, faith, mercy, love; adoption and many others should be addressed accordingly with simplicity. These terms should not in any way be used to intimidate others. Theological and doctrinal themes should be taught with much relevancy. These themes must be practical and life changing. People must see what you are saying, and know where you are going.

Too many churches are lacking when it comes to developing disciples. Every week, prospective parishioners walk down the church aisle to become a part of a major movement in the community. "It is imperative that the church takes the lead and endeavors to remain the spiritual catalyst in guiding individuals and families through the instruction of the Word."[18] Plain and simple, there is the need to get back to basic church training. Many individuals and families are seeking a church to provide them with discipleship training, which meets the needs of all family members.

It is my belief that every ministry in the local church should focus on developing the best disciples for every specific ministry. In order for that to happen, sincere attention must be on the Word. Paul encourages Timothy to handle God's Word correctly. "Do your best to present yourself to God as one approved, a workman who does not need to be ashamed and who correctly handles the word of truth" (2 Timothy 2:15). Every disciple must be a serious student of the Word. I am not saying that we need to be technicians, but we should at least know our direction. Regardless of what our ministries are, we are obligated to be the best disciples for Christ.

It is well said by Jerry Stubblefield in his book, *A Church Ministering to Adults*, "discipleship training should endeavor to strengthen or help the believer be a more effective Christian."[19] Every new disciple and even those who are seasoned saints should know how to help others develop. Authentic discipleship is geared to reaching out to others to help them to become better disciples by training them how to disciple others. Rick Warren, in his book, *The Purpose Driven Church*, states, "Churches grow deeper through discipleship."[20] Every disciple should be eager to be willing to be taught and trained for personal development. In all phases of church growth, through discipleship, we develop a stronger intimacy with God. Intimacy is our total relationship with God. Intimacy is the core of our spiritual growth and development. It is what keeps each of us connected to God.

The church should advocate a strong campaign to encourage individuals to think like disciples, act like disciples, and talk like disciples. If the church is not experiencing a fresh start through discipleship, then serious evaluation must take place. The church must take the initiative in keeping track of its ministries and individuals and to monitor what they are doing in the name of the church. People can't do things in the name of the church without the church having authorized such interaction.

Component Two

Frangelism

The term frangelism is a term that has been taken from the acronym FRAN, which means Friends, Relatives, Associates and Neighbors. This method of evangelism is really for those who may have a hard time doing evangelism. Everyone have individuals who are in every category of the acronym. There should not be any excuse for not sharing salvation with those who are lost. There are too many opportunities that have gone by because the church has been silent. Thousands of people have died and have not had the plan of salvation shared with them. Many of them passed the church daily, weekly, monthly and yearly. Some of them perhaps have been in the church, and still missed the opportunity.

Frangelism could be initiated in so many places, such as: barber shops, beauty salons, malls, picnics, family reunions, camping trips, Christian bookstores, airplanes, cruises, subways, trains, and many others places. Disciples should be able to discern whether a person is ready to receive salvation. While in these places, it should not be the motive of the person who plans to share to disrespect these places by getting into arguments with those who do not desire to hear, in those cases respect the person's rights. In that case, the best that can be done is to pray for the person. Frangelism is not a gimmick to get people who are close to you to hear the gospel, but it is a golden opportunity to present Christ.

This does not mean that those who do not know Christ are not welcomed in the church, which is a great step toward assimilation. What they see, hear and experience will determine where they will end up. Everyone in this group, Friends, Relatives, Associates and Neighbors may be in church but are unchurched. When people are unchurched, it means that they have not yet been assimilated into the life of the church and have not developed a relationship with Jesus.

Lee Strobel, the author of the best selling book, *Inside the Mind of Unchurched Harry and Mary,* wrote: "Almost everyday, we come to evangelistic turning points. We make choices whether to help rescue these people from danger or to walk the other way. We make spur-of-the-moment decisions whether to heroically venture into their lives and lead them to a place of spiritual safety or to merely hope that someone else will do it."[21]

Strobel wrote his book with passion, pride and persuasion. It is true that we as Christians have a vast amount of opportunities to win the unchurched. The unchurched is really Harry and Mary. Harry and Mary are common names to identify the unchurched in so many places. Some church may want to use George and Sandra or Willie and Claudia. Harry and Mary could be the elite, well to do or just plain people. They are just working people who have no interest in the church until they are convinced that Christ is the answer. Harry and Mary could be hard to win. As stated earlier, we come into contact with people from different businesses, but many of us do not seize the moment when it comes to evangelism. We let them go without introducing them to eternal happiness, which is the eternal family of God.

There are those who are in sales, network marketing and other business opportunities who are not shy when it comes to building his or her business. They will give people their business cards, make approaches, get names, appointments and even talk to them right on the spot to convince them to take a look at their product. This is what I call economic evangelism. There is nothing wrong with talking with people, because one can have a prospect list to talk about Jesus at some point. Jesus during his ministry saw the harvest as being ripe. He was not hung up on just his own culture because He had a multi-cultural approach to ministry. He was always on the go and he never gave up on people. He had a tailor made solution for each situation. The main thing was to get people's attention.

> As Jesus approached Jericho, a blind man was sitting by the roadside begging. When he heard the crowd going by, he asked what was happening. They told him, "Jesus of Nazareth is passing by." He called out, "Jesus, Son of David, have mercy on me!"
>
> Those who led the way rebuked him and told him to be quiet, but he shouted all the more, "Son of

David, have mercy on me!" Jesus stopped and ordered the man to be brought to him. When he came near, Jesus asked him, "What do you want me to do for you?" "Lord, I want to see," he replied.

Jesus said to him, "Receive your sight; your faith has healed you." Immediately he received his sight and followed Jesus, praising God. When all the people saw it, they also praised God.[22]

This encounter takes place at a crucial time in Jesus' ministry. He had already identified with those who had been sick. He had ministered in Samaria and Galilee.

It is obvious that the writer says, "Then it happened that as He was coming near Jericho." Jericho was near other places He had to travel. Jesus knew that there was a blind man there begging who needed help. Jericho was a place that Jesus knew was in need. In fact, Jericho was a place that Jesus intended to go. Others may have overlooked Jericho, but not Jesus. Jericho was a place that was not popular, but for Jesus it was a place of priority. He had things there to do. His work was not done until He passed through the town of Jericho.

Today, people need to go through their neighborhoods that are deplorable and run down. Those neighborhoods that are in these conditions are crying out for help. There are those who are in their own culture who will not go in these neighborhoods.

There are African Americans and others who will not go in certain white neighborhoods, as well as some whites who will not go in the African-American or other neighborhoods. They avoided close contact in these neighborhoods, but will witness to them in another part of town, such as the mall or the grocery store.

Jesus did not mind traveling to Jericho. As a matter of fact, Jericho was a place for the disciples to see first hand what real ministry was all about. It was the best place for on the job training for ministry. Jesus did not stop with one situation, He had other encounters. The purpose of His ministry was to merge with as many as possible to deliver them from sin and trouble. Now Jesus decided to demonstrate another personal encounter in Jericho. As soon as Jesus had finished one episode, another one was readily waiting. During his interaction with them, he was showing love and compassion.

He entered Jericho and was passing through. And there was a man named Zacchaeus; he was a chief tax collector, and rich. And he sought to see who Jesus was, but could not, on account of the crowd, because he was small of stature. So he ran on ahead and climbed up into a sycamore tree to see him, for he was to pass that way. And when Jesus came to the place, he looked up and said to him, "Zacchaeus, make haste and come down; for I must stay at your house today." So he made haste and came down, and received him joyfully. [23]

This event in Jesus' ministry was viewed harshly from critics. Many of them could not see Jesus going home with a person such as Zacchaeus. He was the tax collector and he controlled the community. Take note that Luke said that Zacchaeus "climbed up a sycamore tree." He wanted to be sure to see Jesus, but Jesus would have not seen him if he had not climbed up the tree. When one is destined to meet Jesus, it does not matter where he or she may be.

The fact of the matter was that Jesus took that route just

to meet Zacchaeus. In every one of Jesus' crowds, he has a plan for a special situation in the life of someone. The crowd was tight and people had been with him during his healings and teaching. The crowd did not know the reason why Jesus took time to go to Zacchaeus' house. Notice that Jesus invited himself to go home with Zacchaeus. Jesus told him to come down, because he knew the intention of his heart.

There are many in the church today with the mind-set of Zacchaeus. They are short in spiritual height, and desire to see Jesus. They will do all they can to see Jesus. They know Jesus will soon come their way. Today people may climb mental sycamore trees to see Jesus, which means that they have their minds set on Jesus. They have blocked out everything else because they are curious about meeting Jesus. Jesus knows the very intent of people hearts. He knows how excited one can be to see him by the way one act and interacts with others. When this happens, Jesus is on his way into a person's heart to abide with him or her. Today's church should be sensitive to the way people act. Helping people who are hurting requires us to be alert.

It can be a challenge for believers to observe people when they are hurting, depressed, lonely and frustrated. We make the choice to focus on our own problems while leaving others to worry about how they are going to make it. There is the need to be alert in the times in which we live. I have many times become mesmerized in my own circumstances until I forget to really think about others. I admit that that was a mistake because I was so heavily burdened with personal problems.

Since believers are in the same family of God, praises the

same God, we have the tendency to look out for each other. However, Jesus did not intend for us to just look out for ourselves, but have the care and concern for the unchurched. The harvest is running over with people from all walks of life. Their lives are loaded with personal problems. They just do not have a sin problem, but there are other problems, which plague the very fiber of their being. The Bible says, "Share each other's troubles and problems, and in this way obey the law of Christ" (Galatians 6:2, NLT). These burdens are so many and are classified in the context of pain. Christians can help bring relief to a hurting harvest.

Jesus was concerned because he had a ministry, mission and method for combating the very perils of society. He was among the people with their circumstances and situations. He walked with them and discovered what they were looking for. His ministry would be classified as a *ministry of humility*. There was nothing that he would not do, and places he would not go. His driving force was to provide service. The Bible says, "For even the Son of Man did not come to be served, but to serve, and to give his life as a ransom for many" (Mark 10:45).

Those who are in the harvest or unchurched are not really that easy to reach. We have to talk their language, feel their pain, cry with them and seek to understand their world. If we fail to connect with them, we will lose them and they may end up confused in an unchristian atmosphere. If this happens, it will be harder to connect with them and rescue them from the harvest. Where there is no connection, there is no confession, where there is no confession, there is no commitment and where there is no commitment, there is no community.

I remember at one time I had the opportunity to connect with someone who had been hurting. I was reluctant because of their religious affiliation. I kept procrastinating until God allowed the opportunity to resurface again. I asked God to lead me in that situation, which led to an evangelistic moment. The results were that the person accepted Jesus, and is now a viable, dependable, believer. I encourage each of you to take each opportunity serious when God opens a door to help someone who may be hurting.

Let us take a look at another incidence in which Jesus ministered:

> After Jesus crossed over by boat, a large crowd met him at the seaside. One of the meeting-place leaders named Jairus came. When he saw Jesus, he fell to his knees, beside himself as he begged, "My dear daughter is at death's door. Come and lay hands on her so she will get well and live." Jesus went with him, the whole crowd tagging along, pushing and jostling him.
>
> A woman who had suffered a condition of hemorrhaging for twelve years—a long succession of physicians had treated her, and treated her badly, taking all her money and leaving her worse off than before—had heard about Jesus. She slipped in from behind and touched his robe. She was thinking to herself, "If I can put a finger on his robe, I can get well." The moment she did it, the flow of blood dried up. She

could feel the change and knew her plague was over and done with.[24]

This story begins with Jesus on his way to a little girl who was sick. This is a double-miracle in the context of human pain exemplified the passion of pastoral care for both Jarius and the woman with the issue of blood. While he was on his way, and with the crowd increasing heavily, Jesus encountered a woman who had been to every doctor in her time. This woman had a serious blood disease and gravely needed help, hope and healing. The focus was not on the crowd, but it was on the woman. He was not overlooking Jarius' request regarding his daughter, but was impressed with the woman who risked her faith to get to Jesus. Her request was the prelude to deliver Jarius' daughter from death. The focus was to alert the crowd as well as Jarius about healing from heaven. He did not delay his travel but knew that she would desire to be healed. Jesus could have healed her without her pressing her way through the crowd, but it was not meant to be that way. He could have met with her privately. Her healing was not just for her, but for many others in the crowd. They needed to hear what had happened to one who had tried everything.

How Do We Handle Situations When Everything Else Has Failed?

Jesus was dealing with social stimuli, crises and even religious piety. All of this did not distract his mission. He was well prepared to meet the woman who had been sick as well as to raise Jarius' daughter. He was working for the glory of God in order to touch the crowd because there were some critics in the crowd. He knew this woman's intension was real. All she needed was to touch Jesus.

If the truth is to be told, many times we have exhausted all of our resources getting advice from doctors, lawyers, social workers, pastors, marriage counselors, family members, friends, neighbors, and even co-workers. Non-believers, or even those who are skeptics, or atheists will not think about what God can do through Jesus until someone shows them compassion and tender loving care.

It is impossible to deny that the harvest is ripe when so many are crying out for tender loving care. They need to be ministered to. The models that Jesus demonstrates are great models for reaching out to people who are looking for wholeness. As stated earlier, the harvest is ripe before our eyes. It is so ripe until people are falling down before us; they are walking right beside us, sitting beside us, eating with us and we are caught up in our own destiny. They give us clues regarding their lifestyle and sometimes we miss it. The harvest is Christ-centered care because this is what Jesus requires the church to do. Let's see how Jesus responded to the rest of the story:

> At the same moment, Jesus felt energy discharging from him. He turned around to the crowd and asked, "Who touched my robe?" His disciples said, "What are you talking about? With this crowd pushing and jostling you, you're asking, "Who touched me? Dozens have touched you!"
>
> But he went on asking, looking around to see who had done it. The woman, knowing what had happened, knowing she was the one, stepped up in fear

and trembling, knelt before him, and gave him the whole story.

Jesus said to her, "Daughter, you took a risk of faith, and now you're healed and whole. Live well, live blessed! Be healed of your plague."[25]

Jesus was moving through the crowd and observing what had happened when He was touched. He knew someone touched Him because the power of love went from Him. When He queried the crowd regarding who touched Him, they became sarcastic, "why would you ask a question like that when so many are around you, certainly someone touched you."

Helping Someone Requires Sensitivity

If the church is to really respond to the needs of people the way Jesus did, we have to feel their pain and be sensitive to their extenuating circumstances. Jesus made sure He pointed out that He knew what happened. He made the woman aware that he had already noted her case and was on it. He congratulated her regarding her expressed faith. She risked all she had, because she had nothing else to lose. Her back was against the wall and she probably felt like a ton of bricks was on her.

Jesus did not ask for a dissertation regarding her past life and how she found him. He did not put her through red tape. She did not have to fill out any forms, or go through formality. He immediately confirmed in her that she was healed. He gave her His blessings and guaranteed that she would not be plagued by this disease anymore. In fact, she was healed before He asked who touched Him.

Many churches and individuals sometimes do not know

how to respond when someone is trying to get attention. Sometimes we are not fully prepared to handle situations that require sensitivity and compassion. This is a growing edge for the church. We have to know how to encourage those who have expressed faith in Christ. In reality, it should make us happy and we should praise God for the work of faith. While in the harvest when we find someone who desires to be healed of whatever is their issue, the mission is to encourage them to live by faith.

There are those who will not get in the crowd, but will sit on the sidelines waiting for their opportunity. They don't want to be seen by the crowd. This requires the ministry of a few, two or three. As busy as we are, we need to be available to people when they need a touch of love. In contrast, a good example is found with Lazarus' story. The Bible says, "Meanwhile a large crowd of Jews found out that Jesus was there and came, not only because of him but also to see Lazarus, whom he had raised from the dead" (John 12:9).

There are those who are touching us while we are in the crowd, we just have to be sensitive to their touch. This is to say that churches should be open to understanding the cultural context of the unsaved. It is not wise to judge people and decide where they fit in society or the church.

George G. Hunter, III strongly believes:

> "That many traditional churches, by contrast are essentially judgmental towards lost secular people. Many others seem to be motivated by the need to recruit more members to help stop the decline, or pay the bills, or maintain the institutional church. Those are all understandable motives, but compas-

sion drives churches to more authentic outreach and attracts many more seekers toward the faith and the faith community." [26]

The unchurched may respond to the church in different ways. The church really needs a viable authentic outreach ministry. Jesus was on target while ministering to the woman with the blood problem. He was not concerned about the secular, but concerned about the sacredness of meeting divine appointments. Therefore, people need to be trained to connect to the unsaved and implement heart-felt compassion when God paves the way for divine appointments.

Bill Bright & James O. Davis stress the importance of this ministry:

> "As recipients of God's love and compassion, we must reflect that love to the world as well. An apathetic church does not care what is going on around it, forgetting that it was love that first brought its members to Christ. It is more concerned about its own needs and the needs of others. We must pray that God will remove our insensitivity to the hurts of others and make us aware of community needs.[27]

The love of God warms the hearts of believers towards being sensitive to those who are hurting and lost. It compels us to make necessary steps to sharing the Gospel with as many families and individuals. We must remember, that working in the harvest is an investment for the Kingdom, and a blessing for the believer.

Jesus' next encounter with the healing of Jarius' daughter marks a new twist. This comes after he had finished his mission with the woman who had touched his garment. The next significant point came when the men from Jarius' house approached Jairus:

> While Jesus was still speaking, some men came from the house of Jairus, the synagogue ruler. "Your daughter is dead," they said. "why bother the teacher any more?" Ignoring what they said, Jesus told the synagogue ruler, "Don't be afraid; just believe."[28]

Jarius was encouraged to step out on mere Faith. Jesus was turning the focus to believing and not relying on what was said by the skeptics. The men tried to leave and indelible mark in his mind, discrediting the ministry of the master. Jesus insisted that he not be afraid. Being afraid is the work of Satan, which is fear. When Jesus raised Jarius' daughter from the dead it brought hope to those who were lost and shock to the skeptics. Jesus was not trying to impress the skeptics but he was informing them with the power from God.

We will meet all kinds of people in the harvest who have a variety of problems. Some problems are death, sickness, tragedies, depression, etc. Many of them come with doubt because they have not had a Christ encounter. When they are skeptical, we must inform them without debating or arguing. All we have to do is state the claim of the gospel and be natural.

Subsequently, we will encounter some who have been influenced by atheists and others who are adamant against God and being anti-Christian. When the church finds those who are afraid to launch out into the depths of faith, the Word of God must be given to them in order for them to have hope. This means that believers must have a deep faith in Jesus in order to encourage others to live by faith.

As Jesus ended this mission, he wrapped it up in this manner:

> He did not let anyone follow him except Peter, James and John the brother of James. When they came to the home of the synagogue ruler, Jesus saw a commotion, with people crying and wailing loudly. He went in and said to them, "Why all this commotion and wailing? The child is not dead but asleep." But they laughed at him. After he put them all out, he took the child's father and mother and the disciples who were with him, and went in where the child was. He took her by the hand and said to her, "Talitha koum!" (which means, "Little girl, I say to you, get up!"). Immediately the girl stood up and walked around (she was twelve years old). At this they were completely astonished. He gave strict orders not to let anyone know about this, and told them to give her something to eat.[29]

In the context of Jairus' encounter, Jesus took it to another level of spirituality. He knew in advance the status quo of the non-faith community. Jesus made a case out of this encounter. The case was: God worked through Jesus to bring about a change and made a difference for people. In reality they did not know what to do, because they did not know the healer and the Savior. Again I stress the importance of not using those who are relentless and have no biblical and theological foundation relative to their faith journey. These kinds of people will make havoc of the work of Christ. As believers, we must be sensitive and show people how much love heaven has for a troubled world.

After our Lord saw that the people had made such a commotion, He attempted to relax them when He said that the little girl is not dead, but asleep. When He said that she was not dead, He was saying that her death is just a temporary sleep. He also was saying that there will be a resurrection before the resurrection. It will happen here today before your eyes. They were too busy laughing at Him and trying to discredit and dishonor His ministry, until they missed out on the compassion of His ministry. When there is time to give God the glory, we can't be distracted with bystanders and those who have no connection to *The Jesus Movement*. God was at work and there was no time for foolishness. The work of the Kingdom was in process through this little girl. God also used this encounter to leave a message of hope with Mr. Jairus, his wife as well as His disciples. Jesus took them with Him to the little girl. Christ charged them not to tell anyone about what had happened.

This miracle was designed to leave the skeptics wondering because they had no faith. It was a spiritual cliff-hanger which would lead to another episode of healing at some other time. The skeptics could not say anything to Jesus because He put them out. Anytime we are on a divine mission, we can't become involved or argue with those who will try to kill our mission. This is when we have to do as the Bible says, "I am sending you like lambs into a pack of wolves. So be as wise as snakes and as innocent as doves" (Matthew 10:16, CEV). We have to make sure that we stay with God while we work for God. The message from the raising of Jarius' daughter was that there is nothing too hard for God. This takes me to a contrasting story regarding how Jesus handled another sensitive situation. God's will was done and Jarius was glad to see his daughter again.

Compassion in a Time of a Crisis

I am sure that many of us can admit that while we were busy, someone sent word to us to tell us that someone was gravely sick in the hospital, and when we decided to go to see them it was too late. In the case of Jesus with the family of Lazarus, it was never too late. Jesus really invested in the harvest. It must be made clear that Jesus was on a special mission in the case of Lazarus. He had His disciples with him. Here is an important situation regarding Lazarus:

> Now a man named Lazarus was sick. He was from Bethany, the village of Mary and her sister Martha. This Mary, whose brother Lazarus now lay sick, was the same one who poured perfume on the Lord and wiped his feet with her hair. So the sisters sent word to Jesus, "Lord, the one you love is sick." When he heard this, Jesus said, "This sickness will not end in death. No, it is for God's glory so that God's Son may be glorified through it." Jesus loved Martha and her sister and Lazarus. Yet when he heard that Lazarus was sick, he stayed where he was two more days. [30]

This scene with the death of Lazarus is perhaps one of the most intriguing events related to a ripe harvest. There was a need to respond to a situation that did not seem to have any hope. There was a bigger picture than Lazarus. Jesus was not in anyway overlooking the sickness of Lazarus. It would seem that Jesus would rush over to see about Lazarus, but he knew that his sickness would not end in death. It was God's glory because those who had little or no faith could witness God at work. Mary and Martha were thinking about Lazarus' death when God was thinking about deliverance for those who were bound.

Before We Can Show Compassion to Someone, We Must Really Love and Care About Them

Relationships are important. They are important because relationships are built upon trust. Mary and Martha trusted Jesus entirely. Jesus was not only concerned about Lazarus, but Mary and Martha as well. Jesus made a choice to stay where He was two more days. Two more days surely made Mary and Martha nervous and curious about Jesus' compassion. Jesus' motive was to build their faith in Him and God. We can learn from what it means to wait and trust God when things do not seem to really work out.

Notice that Jesus did not hurry. He did not hurry because He had a divine plan for a human situation. His mission in Jerusalem was not over, although He could have changed the course of nature because He was God's Son. He took advantage of the time He had to finish ministering in Jerusalem. His purpose was to reveal the power of God through the death of Lazarus. God's purpose was deeper than Lazarus' sickness and death. Jesus now affirms His mission as He directs His disciples:

> Then he said to his disciples, "Let us go back to Judea."
>
> "But Rabbi," they said, "a short while ago the Jews

tried to stone you, and yet you are going back there?" Jesus answered, "Are there not twelve hours of daylight? A man who walks by day will not stumble, for he sees by this world's light. It is when he walks by night that he stumbles, for he has no light." After He had said this, He went on to tell them, "Our friend Lazarus has fallen asleep; but I am going there to wake him up." His disciples replied, "Lord, if he sleeps, he will get better." Jesus had been speaking of his death, but His disciples thought He meant natural sleep.[31]

As the scene continues, Jesus wanted His disciples to understand the following as they had to understand another level of discipleship:

So then he told them plainly, "Lazarus is dead, and for your sake I am glad I was not there, so that you may believe. But let us go to him." Then Thomas (called Didymus) said to the rest of the disciples, "Let us also go, that we may die with him." On His arrival, Jesus found that Lazarus had already been in the tomb for four days. Bethany was less than two miles from Jerusalem, and many Jews had come to Martha and Mary to comfort them in the loss of their brother. When Martha heard that Jesus was coming, she went out to meet him, but Mary stayed at home.[32]

Jesus had to be candid with His disciples regarding the status of Lazarus. True discipleship is stating the facts regarding any circumstance or situation. Jesus wanted His disciples to really see what God could do through Him. The point here is that

Thomas was a doubter. When one responds to the harvest, one cannot respond out of fear. There must be total trust in Jesus. There are too many doubting Thomases in churches today. Jesus was trying to redirect the focus of the disciples. Here is a lesson for us:

We should learn that it is important to glorify God in the midst of skeptics and doubters

As it was in New Testament times, we need to have complete faith in God when we have to inspire others to believe. Before we can introduce Jesus to those who have a faith problem, we need to know Him. There are many who are blind because Satan does not want God's people to display absolute faith in the midst of doubt.

Thomas had a negative remark to convey to the rest of the disciples regarding Jesus' ministry. Thomas had given up and he desired to die and invite others also. In other words, Thomas was saying that the other disciples should not follow Jesus because He could not even go and heal Lazarus. He was saying that Jesus was a failure. Jesus did not respond to his negative response. The master just kept on traveling until He came to the place where Lazarus was laid. Because Lazarus was dead four days, they thought all hope was gone.

Another one of Jesus' purposes was to comfort Mary and Martha during their bereavement. They were in a false bereavement but they did not know that. They were not aware that a miracle was going to happen. Martha heard that Jesus was coming, so she prepared herself to meet Him. She met Him because she was curious to see what would happen. Look how Martha responded to Jesus:

> "Then Martha said to Jesus, "Lord, if you had been here, my brother would not have died. But I know that even now God will give you whatever you ask." Jesus said to her, "Your brother will rise again." Martha answered, "I know he will rise again in the resurrection at the last day." Jesus said to her, "I am the resurrection and the life. He who believes in me will live, even though he dies; and whoever lives and believes in me will never die. Do you believe this?" "Yes, Lord," she told him, "I believe that you are the Christ, the Son of God, who was to come into the world."[33]

Martha made her way to Jesus. She could not wait to talk to Him. She immediately told Jesus how she felt about Him and how much faith she had in Him. Martha was not a doubter. What she was saying was that Jesus had the answer for her brother. She said, "If you had been here, my brother would not have died." How many do we come in contact with can say this with firmness. This is really a statement of honor because Martha respects Jesus highly because He was a friend of the family. She was disappointed because Jesus did not come in time. What was important was that Jesus was there for her to comfort her beyond what she could ever imagine. As disciples today, we have to comfort others regardless of their plight. As the church today approaches the harvest, we really need more Marthas who really believe in Jesus and can give encouragement. There are many Lazaruses who are already dead spiritually and need to be resurrected. There are many Marthas,

Part 2: The Harvest Factor

Marys and Lazaruses in the harvest that need the attention of the church.

There are new Christians who need someone just to care for them. They have been waiting for a long time to be rescued from their discomfort. When mature Christians have to go and minister to those who are in the harvest, encouragement is needed in order for evangelism to be effective. Many times comfort is needed for those who are going to comfort others. Responding to the harvest is about bringing the gospel to a wide variety of people. This means that the gospel is not relegated to one or two cultures, but to everyone. The harvest could be in any corner of the community or society. "For as long as there have been Christians with a zeal to bring the good news of salvation to unreached peoples in sundry parts of the world, there have been different ideas as to how to tackle this evangelistic task."[34]

There are those who are ready to be trained to go in the harvest to tackle the task of evangelism and help disciple people from all walks of life. Knowing how to handle people is a gift from God. Jesus knew how to handle whatever he encountered. He was not worried about Martha because he had the prescription for her discomfort. Here is how this scene unfolded:

> And after she had said this, she went back and called her sister Mary aside. "The Teacher is here," she said, "and is asking for you." When Mary heard this, she got up quickly and went to him. Now Jesus had not yet entered the village, but was still at the place where Martha had met him. When the Jews who had been with Mary in the house, comforting

her, noticed how quickly she got up and went out, they followed her, supposing she was going to the tomb to mourn there. When Mary reached the place where Jesus was and saw him, she fell at his feet and said, "Lord, if you had been here, my brother would not have died."

When Jesus saw her weeping, and the Jews who had come along with her also weeping, He was deeply moved in spirit and troubled. "Where have you laid him?" he asked. "Come and see, Lord," they replied. Jesus wept. Then the Jews said, "See how he loved him!" But some of them said, "Could not he who opened the eyes of the blind man have kept this man from dying?"[35]

After Mary was informed that Jesus was in the area, she quickly went to him. She went weeping because she really loved her brother, Lazarus. Her response was the same as her sister Martha, Mary just believed if Jesus had been there Lazarus would not have died. Her response was more intense than her sister. Jesus was touched by her weeping and began to bring her grief to an end. He was not worried about the Jews, but He just wanted to know where they have laid him. There are many in the harvest lying around waiting to be resurrected from bondage, low–self esteem, and depression.

While working in the harvest we must be prepared to face criticisms. They come from many directions. However, our theological stance with God is that we must keep our sanity. The Jews gave Jesus credit for opening the eyes of the blind, but discredited Him regarding healing Lazarus. The Jews were not aware as well as others what God had in mind regarding the Lazarus Miracle. The story of Lazarus was about faith. Let us close in on the remainder of the scene at the tomb:

> Jesus, once more deeply moved, came to the tomb. It was a cave with a stone laid across the entrance. "Take away the stone," he said. "But, Lord," said Martha, the sister of the dead man, "by this time there is a bad odor, for he has been there four days." Then Jesus said, "Did I not tell you that if you believed, you would see the glory of God?" So they took away the stone. Then Jesus looked up and said, "Father, I thank you that you have heard me. I knew that you always hear me, but I said this for the benefit of the people standing here, that they may believe that you sent me."
>
> When he had said this, Jesus called in a loud voice, "Lazarus, come out!" The dead man came out, his hands and feet wrapped with strips of linen, and a cloth around his face. Jesus said to them, "Take off the grave clothes and let him go."[36]

Jesus intended to wait until the right time to respond to Martha and Mary. Lazarus was stinking now and the Jews that were at the tomb were not expecting Jesus to really do anything. This is what goes on during the harvest. There are those who are standing around the present day disciples of Christ waiting for things to go wrong. What happened to Martha's faith? She thought that her brother had been dead too long, and that it was over because he has had an odor.

Jesus' emphasis now was to minister to Mary and Martha because things did not look so good for them. It seems as though Martha and Mary had been focusing more on their sorrow rather than their salvation. It was bad enough being in the presence of others who had doubts. The real harvest is responding when we hear the call and cry of the wounded that need healing. Sometimes some will not be healed because God's purpose is for their faith to grow during their moment of sickness.

Because of who Jesus is, He could have spoken a miracle into existence and hushed the mouths of the Jews. He could have baffled critics and put them into mere wonder as a result of their curiosity. Jesus' disciples experienced first hand what to do in the harvest when the odds were stacked against them. All Jesus did was prayed to His father for divine intervention in the midst of doubt, sarcasm and skepticism. The church today must never worry about what will happen in the harvest, but look at the possibilities of bringing closure and hope to the lives of those like Martha and Mary.

STUDY REVIEW GUIDE: RESPONDING TO THE HARVEST

Biblical Truth

Believers are commissioned for field work.

Key Word

BEAR: The Greek word for bear is *phero* which means to carry or bring. The word is pronounced as fer'-o.

Memory Verses

John 15:1–3

Point of Emphasis

It is impossible to deny that the harvest is ripe.

Theological Reflection

Your theological views and reflection from this study.

Personal Application

Your thoughts on how this study has impacted you.

Study Questions

1. What is the harvest?

2. Why is evangelism the key focus of the Great Commission?

3. Who are Harry and Mary?

4. How does the biblical truth relate to your ministry?

5. What lesson do we learn from Jesus and the Samaritan Woman?

THE RESULTS OF HARVEST WORK

GROWING A HEALTHY CHURCH

> "And we pray this in order that you may live a life worthy of the Lord and may please him in every way: bearing fruit in every good work, growing in the knowledge of God, being strengthened with all power according to his glorious might so that you may have great endurance and patience, and joyfully giving thanks to the Father, who has qualified you to share in the inheritance of the saints in the kingdom of light" (Colossians 1:10–12).

Growing healthy disciples is the answer to church growth.

The heart of a healthy church depends largely on those who are serious concerning the focus of discipleship. Discipleship is a necessity and not an option. It is a responsibility, which is clearly stated in the New Testament. In order for the church to really reach individuals and prepare them for ministry, there must be a clear cut understanding of what discipleship means, especially as we are now is a new millennium.

Growing a healthy church is focusing on spiritual maturity and not numbers. Authentic church health is monitoring how each person is progressing in regard to his or her relationship with God. Evidence of maturity is based on a person's conviction, conversation and character. Conviction is associated with faith. Conversation is associated with boldness, and character is associated with lifestyle. Spiritual maturity is necessary for each believer to walk and stand strong with God. One cannot fully experience God and enjoy his presence without growing spiritually. The focus of this chapter is on growing the disciples who are in the local church. This is because they already have a relationship; it just needs to be stronger. In order to grow new disciples, the church must have strong disciples who are ready to launch out and help others.

In the Gospel of Matthew Jesus lays the foundation for the mandate for developing disciples for a healthy ministry. "Go therefore and make disciples of all the nations, baptizing them in the name of the Father and of the Son and of the Holy Spirit, teaching them to observe all things that I have commanded you; and lo, I am with you always, even to the end of the age" (28:19–20). I will focus on seven principles for developing a viable and healthy discipleship ministry:

1. Counting the Cost of Discipleship

2. Keeping Disciples Healthy

3. Restoring and Rebuilding Through Training
4. The Need for Spirit–filled Disciples
5. Developing Disciples through Mentoring
6. The Necessity of Management
7. Duplicating Disciples for Development.

These principles or methods are not intended to adequately answer the many questions about discipleship. However, the motive for these principles is to raise the conscious of parishioners and encourage them to have high expectations for developing quality disciples that will make a difference for effective soul winning. The church must take control of soul winning and not allow Satan to win.

Counting the Cost of Discipleship

In order for the church to maximize and do justice to the ministry of discipleship, there is a need to have a clear understanding of the cost of discipleship. It is necessary to count the cost. Just what does it cost? It costs something to follow Jesus. The cost is in the word bear. Every encounter we have is related to our cross-bearing. We cannot be ashamed of bearing the cross. (See Mark 9:12). Disciples must be willing to bear the cross. Bearing the cross means to be ready to accept criticisms. The truth of the matter is that more people are wearing a cross instead of bearing the cross. One is able to bear the cross when he or she is healthy. It is therefore necessary to understand what the word disciple means. The word disciple comes from the Greek word *Mathetes*, literally a learner.

A learner is really one who seeks knowledge; a scholar who combines both theory and practice as team partners for effective ministry. It also denotes one who follows which is connected to one who learns. They both go hand-in hand. One who follows is one who is in the process of learning about the Bible, theology, Christian education and church history. All four areas set the stage for developing healthy disciples. A true disciple must model after what Jesus says. In Mark 8:34, Jesus makes it clear concerning what is required of a disciple, "Whoever desires to come after Me, let him deny himself, and follow Me." Following Jesus is costly.

There is nothing cheap about discipleship. If discipleship is to reach its goal, then it is necessary to count the cost. This means just what is expected of each disciple. The real cost of discipleship is to do more than just the ordinary for Christ. One must make major sacrifices in order to be a true disciple. Dietrich Bonhoeffer in his book, *The Cost of Discipleship*, states that "When the Bible speaks of following Jesus, it is proclaiming a discipleship which will liberate mankind from all man-made dogmas, from every burden and oppression, from every anxiety and torture which afflicts the conscience."[37] He is specifically focusing on sharing this ministry with everyone and at the same time conveying the message of liberation.

When another person is trained as a new disciple, he or she has become a liberator. Individuals need the church to liberate them from their suffering and pain. Real discipleship is a serious enterprise. It is more serious than the way most churches really view it. Since the cost of discipleship is rising, churches should know the value of discipleship and the responsibilities, which go along with it.

The church needs to invest in preparing individuals to meet the cost of discipleship. Meeting the cost of discipleship is having classes and workshops centered on making disciples for Christ. The sky is the limit as to where the church can go when quality discipleship is in operation.

When there is quality discipleship, there is healthy discipleship. I agree with Rick Warren when he states in his book, *The Purpose Driven Church,* that "a balanced church will be a healthy church."[38] This means that the people must have a plan of action designed to meet the demands of this important ministry. Discipleship must not be exchanged for "discipleslip" (meaning disciples are slipping on the job of spiritual growth). Discipleslip is not a word, but a concept of being lazy.

It is recommended that the action plan outline the strategies, methods and approaches for developing healthy disciples for kingdom building. In reality, disciples are kingdom builders, because this is what Jesus trained us to do, using his disciples as the example for ministry.

Vital Signs that Keep Disciples Healthy

Each member of the Body of Christ must be healthy in order for the entire Body to be healthy. There are vital signs for spiritual maturity. Just as the human body needs all of it parts to function, the spiritual body also must function. The physical body requires a series of examinations during a twelve-month period to keep in check the condition of the body.

Some people go more than others and some don't go at all. Some people shy away from the doctor because of fear. They are afraid of what they might find out. That's not good judgment. Some people go to the doctor regularly and still the doctor can't guarantee progress for their condition, but they faithfully go. Some people don't go the doctor because they don't have medical coverage.

Paul uses the metaphor of the Body of Christ so we could identify with how we function in the Body of Christ. I will mention three ways for staying healthy in the Body of Christ. The first vital sign is worship. Worship brings nurture. This means that one must visit Jesus regularly. Visiting Jesus is really to worship. We must visit Him through meditation. The Body of Christ needs treatment. Treatment is needed daily. The wrong treatment will not help the believer grow into spiritual maturity and maintain excellent spiritual health. One cannot get the right treatment by going after strange doctrine, which are strange teachings.

Strange teaching develops lopsided believers. When one is lopsided, there is neither productivity nor progress in the Body of Christ. This daily treatment keeps the believer spiritually in check. This treatment includes a life of prayer and the study of the scriptures. When we pray, we are exchanging our hurts for God's healing. Jesus stands before God on our behalf, interceding for us daily. If Jesus is doing this for us, why can't we take time out and talk with him, and appreciate his spiritual nurturing. Prayer keeps us focused for the purpose of God's will in our lives.

The second vital sign is to study the Word. Without studying the Word, we have no way of receiving the nutrients that our spiritual body needs. "Like newborn babies crave pure spiritual milk, so that by it you may grow up in your salvation" (1 Peter 2:1–2). It is important that we grow daily. Receiving spiritual vitamins are important for spiritual growth. The third vital sign is to live a life of faith. We must have faith in Jesus. Living by faith means that we fully trust God for everything. There is no substitute for faith.

Restoring and Rebuilding Through Training

There is a need to restore and rebuild basic discipleship training in the church. The way to keep people healthy is through training. This is because in order for the church to remain a viable catalyst in the community and abroad, there must a theological understanding of the meaning of discipleship training. Parishioners cannot move to the next level of training until successfully completing basic training.

Discipleship training gives credibility to both the individual and the church for rebuilding an effective ministry. This credibility is grounded in the person and work of the Holy Spirit to bring about a change in discipleship training. The emphasis and focus is to look at the overall curriculum, which involves discipleship. It focuses on developing and deploying disciples for spiritual survival in every phase of ministry. There must be a cooperative effort of the church to seriously set the stage and recover this needed ministry. Therefore, discipleship training is a direct response to our Christian commitment in fulfilling the Great Commandment.

Being a disciple is no short term adventure; we are disciples for life. Since we are in this for life, then we must work to that end. Our commitment must be to please God in every way possible in terms of discipleship training. Discipleship training should be an exciting ministry in the church as we move toward the next century. This excitement should be geared to get individuals involved in a discipleship class. "Discipleship training is crucial for the growth, development, and maturity of all Christians if they are to grow to Christ likeness and do the work of Christ in the world."[39] When Christians are growing, developing, and maturing, they are recovering and rebuilding the ministry of discipleship. This is one way of being a healthy church. What the church really is doing is going back and reclaiming what was rightfully theirs, rescuing disciples from satanic forces. There is nothing healthy about being a disciple of Satan.

The reason that many churches are not prospering in the ministry of discipleship is because somehow Satan has injected the deadly venom of complacency, preventing the church from growing healthy and responsible disciples. This deadly venom of complacency holds the church hostage and what appears to be discipleship is not. This is because those disciples who are not in some class are not being nurtured for maximum growth. One can also be nurtured on a one on one basis, but even that in some cases are not being fulfilled because of a lack of emphasis on true discipleship.

Therefore, there is a need to restore and rebuild discipleship in all areas of ministry. It is necessary to briefly describe three ministries that are a part of discipleship. (1) Evangelism is a ministry of reaching people through teaching. Every new convert should receive instruction. The apostles were evangelists. Many others were evangelists other than apostles. This is clarified in Ephesians 4:11. There is a need for those specifically in the ministry of evangelism to develop as genuine *evangelistic disciples.* (2) Stewardship is a ministry of accountability and trust. (Luke 16:2, 3,4). God has appointed us as trustees or managers over his household of creation. A good disciple is a good steward. Every new disciple should be instructed on the necessity of being good *stewardship disciples.* (3) Mission work is a ministry of caring. Therefore, every ministry in the church is mission focused. John's gospel states, "Peace be with you! As the Father has sent me, I am sending you" (John: 20:21). In this passage, the word send comes from the Greek word *Pempo,* which means to send. It is a general term and not the same as the Greek word *Apostello,* which means to send in an authoritative manner. Both sometimes are used interchangeably. All disciples are missionaries, ministers and evangelists.

The Need for Spirit-filled Disciples

Being Spirit-filled is being controlled by the Holy Spirit to do ministry as a disciple in the manner in which God intends and directs. When one is Spirit-filled, one is also Spirit-led and Spirit-fed. Jesus did not call his first disciples to be empty, morbid and irresponsible. He called them to a work, a work of righteousness. He called them to be anointed for this work. Spirit-filled disciples mean business, because that is just what God means. When one is Spirit-filled, he or she must encourage others to experience this powerful anointing from God. Every disciple must seek God's anointing for his or her life coupled with discovering his or her spiritual gifts. Spiritual gifts are important for the ministry of discipleship.

It is important because gifts identify one's ministry and how each person can best function in the Body of Christ. Every disciple has been endowed with a gift or gifts, but not all of the gifts of the Spirit.

Peter shares a positive principle regarding how to use a special gift, "As each one has received a special gift, employ it in serving one another, as good stewards of the manifold grace of God" (1 Peter 4:10). A disciple who is not employing his or her special gift is short-circuiting his or her spirituality and is an embarrassment to the Body of Christ. In these times, we need more dedicated and Spirit–filled disciples who are not lazy but are willing to make good use of their gift. Every disciple has "a charge to keep and a God to Glorify." The truth of the matter is that we are called to the ministry of discipleship. Therefore, we must allow the Spirit to use all of our talents for the glory of God.

The emphasis concerning Spirit–filled disciples presupposes that there is a lack of Spirit–filled disciples in the church. Evidence of this is revealed in the lack of individuals in churches who are not experiencing Christian growth. We should "grow in the grace and knowledge of our Lord and Savior Jesus Christ" (2 Peter 3:18). Churches should develop and implement a mission statement for discipleship. The mission statement should emphasize the need for Spirit–filled and Spirit-led disciples. Spirit–filled disciples should encourage other disciples to employ their special gift. There is not enough emphasis on Spiritual gifts. The use of Spiritual gifts has become silent in many churches, and for those reasons, those churches have become stagnant and docile.

It is my opinion that this exists because individuals have

not discovered what their gift is. "As we train young Christians to become disciples, one of our primary objectives should be to help them discover and develop their gifts. Since every believer has gifts, which God holds him accountable for developing and using for the sake of the body."[40] Discovering gifts clear the way for a healthy ministry. The threads of a serious discipleship weave a healthy ministry that's endowed by the use of spiritual gifts.

I relish the book by Dale Galloway, *The Small Group.* It is a powerful tool for those who desire to change stagnant and bewildered churches into vibrant healthy churches. Those who have the anointing to organize from the ground up will be blessed to leaf the pages of this book. The best way to develop disciples for the harvest is to realize that "small groups are where people connect with other people, with God, and with the church; they are where heart-to-heart ministry, or "people care"- takes place."[41] When people know that they matter, then they know that what they do for God really matters. This means that they desire to be trained. Cell groups focus on the felt need of the group, and that's really ministering. The harvest can't be reached without the developmental plan of keeping it going and passing it on to the next person prepared and willing to be trained for small group ministry.

A church can forever be equipped with resources and people with skills and abilities. None of this is worth anything unless one develops a close association with others. Jesus definitely made association. There must be meetings. We must show the plan of salvation to prospective disciples repeatedly and get them ready for discipleship and evangelism. Time must be spent with new disciples to assure them that they are in for the ride of their lifetime. They will help others to become Christians. Many are unchurched, and are waiting for the right time for someone to share with them about the exciting news of the Kingdom of God!

I can vividly remember growing up in church in the South and witnessing when new converts came and gave God their heart and the preacher their hand. They were not allowed to go before the church until they had been to the mourner's bench. The purpose of the mourner's bench was for individuals to seek the Holy Ghost over a period of time. New converts were ministered to by the matured saints of the church. Converts had to show evidence of spiritual growth before they could be recommended to the church for membership.

The goal of the church was to nurture them one on one. They were using the small group model without labeling it. The new converts were nurtured during the seeking process. They were given instruction and encouragement. Before the waiting congregation voted new the membership, the church clerk or designee would read the report to the church, which states: "we have Mr. or Mrs._____ who comes to us as a candidate for baptism. The pastor would respond by saying, do you believe in the Lord and Savior Jesus Christ and want to be baptized? The person would say yes. You have heard the report coming from the clerk, what's your pleasure? Someone would offer a motion by saying, "I so move that we would accept the report from the church clerk, and someone would second it." The motion is carried and the person is accepted into the membership with all rights and privileges. This method is exactly how it is done today in some churches. However, it is not necessary today to vote new converts into the church. Therefore, many churches do not use the voting method, they are just accepted.

This method was the epitome of what was at that time discipleship, many years ago. Some pastors asked new converts during their testimony what would they like to do in the church? Some said sing and others mostly said usher, and some, I don't know. The problem with that was that people were spiritually immature and did not know what they wanted to do. They were put where they were needed because people did not know what their spiritual gifts were. People got caught up in the context of church-ship rather than discipleship. Church-ship simply means doing every thing other than growing disciples. Developing and duplicating disciples for the harvest requires commitment and dedication.

Jesus did not spend time on this earth just to be seen and heard. The time He spent with His disciples was for a purpose (Matt: 8: 5–8). He trained them to develop and duplicate others. I am reminded of the paramecium in biology, a single celled animal. When part of the body of the paramecium is separated from the body, the part that was separated reproduces into a new paramecium. There is a need to reproduce disciples who have been cut off or who have become weak. The church really needs to seriously revamp its approach to producing more disciples. Probably, the reason why many churches are weak when it comes to duplicating disciples is because of the lack of commitment and dedication on the part of the church. When we talk about commitment, we mean doing all and more than what is required to get the job done. "The practice of high commitment on the part of leadership is the backbone of the high commitment environment.

If the practices of the church leadership do not support the teaching, the standards will be ignored, and the congregation's commitment will be low."[42]

A good place to build commitment is to start in the cell groups. I consider a cell group a small family or community. It is an opportunity for one to grow spiritually and mature in the faith. Cell groups build confidence and trust while being nurtured. If a person is really going to be committed, it will surface in cell groups. Many people hide behind crowds instead of taking responsibility for their own ministry. In most cases, other individuals carry the load. Some people constantly reject the word, because they don't want to hear and live by the truth. This is because they have a balloon attitude and are wrapped into their own cognitive ignorance. In other words, they feel that there is no or little need for spiritual renewal. Time has to be made for spiritual renewal. Getting close to God should be the believer's primary goal. Therefore, the pastor must equip leaders so they will understand the vision for discipleship and spiritual growth. The key to understanding begins with the following methods:

Developing Disciples through Mentoring

There is no way to develop disciples without taking in the concept of discipleship training. Assimilating discipleship training is patterned after the teachings of Jesus. Those who are trained as disciples should be eager to learn new methods, principles and concepts of training in order to reproduce themselves in others. When churches are able to assimilate the discipleship plan effectively, the church attracts others in a powerful way. This powerful way is mentoring. Mentoring is the same as sponsoring. Mentoring goes hand in hand with building a discipleship church through cell groups.

In some network marketing organizations, the method of sponsorship is the key to success. When one is sponsored, the sponsor is responsible for teaching and training. Christians are obligated to lead and disciple someone else to Christ. Commitment means that the person who is the mentor is committed to helping one grow. There must be a passion to help and encourage others to become true disciples through the mentoring nurturing plan. In like manner as a sponsor, the mentor is responsible for teaching and training new converts. The mentor spends quality time with the mentee, guiding him or her through the process of Christian maturity.

The Necessity of Management

Management is an element of mentoring. It is a way of discipline. Individuals must be well disciplined and not allowing trivial matters to curve them off course. One who is a good mentor is a good manager. Management means to keep a person on track so that he or she will achieve their goals and objectives. It helps one to manage their time schedule and develop a structured routine. It is important as much as possible to help those who are new converts to learn to become disciplined and to manage their time so that they will be effective disciples. Management should be the goal of every leader and individual, because it is crucial in that it requires dedication and structure.

One cannot ask others to be dedicated when in fact they are not. Dedication is not an option, but a necessity. Management does not only require dedication, but discipline as well. If one can manage his or her own spiritual life, then he or she can help and encourage others to do the same. The goal is to encourage every church to think about nurturing.

Developing Disciples for Duplication

There is no need to develop disciples for ministry and not train them how to develop others. The purpose of duplication is to utilize individuals to implement the Great Commission. The church must seek to deploy as many as possible to focus on duplication. Duplication is the local church being extended for the work of the Kingdom. Discipleship is a one–on–one encounter. It is a method of spreading the gospel through individuals. It can't be said enough that discipleship is the ministry of the church and not just the pastor. There is no excuse for not helping the church to duplicate believers as kingdom builders. Almost everything in the church is duplicated except discipleship and evangelism. When one has been duplicated, he or she is equipped for service. This leads us to the second phase of growing a healthy church.

Steps For Nurturing A Healthy Church

There are peaks, slopes and curves during the nurturing process of church growth. There are seven basic steps that I believe will make a difference in any church. They are: (1) Being Totally Committed, (2) Spending Quality Time with God through Meditation, (3) Spending Time in Prayer, (4) Spending Quality Time in the Word, (5) Sharing Your Testimony, (6) Walking by Faith, and (7) Implementing Forgiveness. In order for a church to become healthy, there must

Introduction

be nurturing. Proper nurturing grows the church and keeps the church vivacious. These steps keep the church strong and alert in a difficult world. I believe that every church desires to grow. However, some are more eager than others and by taking the initiative and working hard some can evaluate and know where they are.

Being Totally Committed

The first step to becoming a healthy church is to be totally committed. One has to have the flame of commitment written in his or her heart. It is easy to say how much we love the Lord. Jesus wants our action more than our lips. We can read Matthew 11:28 everyday, and not be committed to what it means is no good. If one does not have a commitment to learn of God, then he or she is not being real. There have been many times that I had to think about my own personal growth as a Christian. God knows about our growth commitment. He hears everything we say and sees everything we do. True commitment gets to the core of our being. Many of us should feel guilty when we are not committed. All of us should think about what Christ says concerning commitment, Jesus replied, "No one who puts his hand to the plow and looks back is fit for service in the kingdom of God" (Luke 9:62). What Jesus is saying is that we can't play around with Kingdom work. The church must provide first–class service which leads to being a five–star church. It takes commitment to move ahead with a purpose and plan regarding the gospel. Right now you may be thinking about how committed you are. No matter how much you think you are, sometimes our commitment is not enough for God. We have to go the extra mile. There is a need to keep trying even when it seems impossible. We need to admit when we have been slack concerning being totally committed and "Put on all of God's armor so that you will be able to stand firm against all strategies and tricks of the Devil" (Ephesians 6:11, NLT). It takes the grace of God to help us to keep our commitment as we become fully armored. In order to nurture disciples, the church must change its course of action and step up when it comes to commitment.

Spending Quality Time With God Through Meditation

Spending time with God means to be in His presence. It is the time of meditation. It is the time that we give Him total devotion. Our devotion should be emerged in the Holy Spirit. If our spirits are low, there can and will be a change. We can leave on a high. If we come empty, He will fill us with His grace. If we come bruised, He will heal our spirits. I believe that the church cannot really nurture people without encouraging them to learn how to spend quality time with God. Time with God means to just listen to what God has to say. We don't need to wait until trouble comes, just to decide to spend time with God. Tommy Tenney, author of *Experiencing His Presence: Devotions for God Catchers,* says, "Human desperation and brokenness are the mortar and stone of heavenly dependence, and they are the integral components of greatness in God. He can use virtually everything that drives us from the limits of our strength, endurance, abilities and resources to draw us closer to His heart and deeper into His purposes."[43] When one spends time with God, there is no doubt that time well spent will not be in vain. Time with God means time with no one else.

Total focus must be on God without any distractions. Nurturing individuals to develop a closer walk with God is a great contribution that the church can make regarding ministry. Time spent with God will certainly strengthen one's life. This leads to the next step.

Spending Time in Prayer

The previous section was on meditation. This section is on prayer. It is prayer time. The church and individuals are to spend quality time in prayer. It's not how long one prays, but what is said. And what is said with a sincere heart will be well pleasing to God. Praying to God means to be honest with God about what's on your mind. Spending time in prayer with God means that it is a constant daily walk. This is the time for an intimate relationship. Here is an incisive question that needs to be answered: How often should we spend time in prayer with God? The Bible says, "Then Jesus told his disciples a parable to show them that they should always pray and not give up" (Luke 18:1). Jesus was telling His disciples no matter what happens, they should never quit praying. If they quit praying they will have no recourse but to give up. A life without prayer is a life on a shaky foundation. It is subject to sink at any time. Sometimes it gets hard and difficult, but prayer is the answer. The more time spent with God in prayer breaks up the connection that Satan tries to make with God's people, keeping them from staying in touch with God.

The more time spent with God in prayer opens the door of God's presence for fresh anointing. This fresh anointing prepares believers for daily activities, events and battles. Another important question is what does it mean to spend time in prayer? Well, it means more than one can imagine. It means having a relationship with God. It means really knowing God and experiencing God. E. M. Bounds, a profound writer on prayer, wrote, "God has everything to do with prayer as well as everything to do with the one who prays."[44] When one prays, God reveals His sacred presence in order to communicate with finite creatures. When God does this, this is grace working in the realm of prayer. We really do not deserve it but because we are disciples trying to grow healthy, God allows us in His presence to communicate with Him. The church must have a desire to encourage those who do not know God to get to know Him and spend time in prayer with Him. Spending time in prayer means to approach God daily and not just in case of emergencies. This means that we must have faith when we pray, whether normal or during an emergency. God is moved more when we approach Him as constant friends who talk with Him daily as oppose to when we have an emergency. It must be known that God certainly works during emergencies. Regardless of what approach we take to God, we must be sincere, and we must thank God at the conclusion of the prayer.

Bill Hybels, a noted author and pastor says this about prayer: "According to the Bible, believers can be confident that their prayers will be answered. Our prayers are more than wishes, hopes or feeble aspirations-but only if we pray with believing, faith-filled hearts. That is the kind of prayer that moves mountains."[45]

I thank God for His blessings and the love He has for

us. The point is that we need to spend more time with God in prayer. Spending time with God means that one is truly sanctified. The word sanctification means to be separated from the world to God. One cannot effectively pray and be separated from God. Prayer must be a significant part of the life of the church. Regardless of social change, the church must have a theological position regarding prayer. People experience many things in life that can affect their relationship with God and impede their time spent with Him. Harold A. Carter says this concerning time spent in prayer with God: "Every church would do well to provide some definite hour for prayer when members are vigorously urged to come out and participate in this service. In this hour, songs of the spirit can burst out anew from the worshipping souls of God's people. God's Word can be taught to enrich the experience of prayer."[46] I concur with Carter in that time should be set aside for prayer. However, too many churches have penciled in a specific time for prayer, but little effort is made to carry out this needed ministry. This is why there needs to be clear minds and clear hearts to prepare for a spiritual and vibrant moment of prayer. God is expecting that all of us spend more time with Him in prayer.

Spending Quality Time in the Word

There is no substitute for replacing the Word of God. A church can't really grow healthy disciples without the Word of God. There is no getting around it, the Word is needed. Spending time in the Word separates disciples from members. One cannot be nurtured without the Word of God. This means that our hope and foundation is on the Word.

I will list some passages that get my attention regarding the Word. Paul affirms his ministry to the Thessalonians regarding the Word of God. In I Thessalonians 2:13, he emphasizes that the "Word is at work in those who believe." This means that when we believe the Word, God blesses. Colossians 3:16 is about the word of Christ. "Let the word of Christ dwell in you richly as you teach and admonish one another with all wisdom, and as you sing psalms, hymns and spiritual songs with gratitude in your hearts to God." This verse is an encouragement to really become focused on the Word. Paul is saying here that the Word has to take root and dwell in your soul and heart. In Acts 13:26, Luke makes reference to the Word of Salvation, and in Romans 10:8, it speaks about the Word of Faith.

Here is a remarkable act of humility on the part of Jesus,

> "Jesus returned to Galilee in the power of the Spirit, and news about him spread through the whole countryside. He taught in their synagogues, and everyone praised him. He went to Nazareth, where he had been brought up, and on the Sabbath day he went into the synagogue, as was his custom. And he stood up to read. The scroll of the prophet Isaiah was handed to him. Unrolling it, he found the place where it is written: "The Spirit of the Lord is on me, because he has anointed me to preach good news to the poor. He has sent me to proclaim freedom for the prisoners and recovery of sight for the blind, to release the oppressed, to proclaim the year of the Lord's favor." Then he rolled up the scroll, gave it back to the attendant and sat down. The eyes of everyone in the

synagogue were fastened on him, and he began by saying to them, "Today this scripture is fulfilled in your hearing." 47

Jesus stood up and read with love and joy in the synagogue. He was setting an example how to be respectable in the House of God. This act of humility really affected people and impacted them. Through His example, they were changed forever. Personally, I have been encouraged by what He did. Jesus was setting the example that we should rely on the Word for our spiritual nurture. Staying in the Word brings the best out of us because we are connected to God and receive God's favor for our destiny. Hear what the Psalmist says, "Forever, O LORD, Your word is settled in heaven" (Psalm 119:89).

Sharing your Testimony

Testimonies are designed to be shared. Your testimony can inspire others to make a decision to accept Jesus and become a disciple. Many times there are others who will never see the glory of God until they see it in believers. God has not allowed any of us to go through testing times for nothing. Many times we are going through some things to bless others. There are those who are ashamed, and maybe ashamed for many reasons. Some may be in situations where they cannot share their testimony.

They may be in a meeting on their job where it might not be appropriate, and this may be true, but when they get the chance, they should. This means that we have to wait until God provides the right moment, and when that happens, we should seize it. Another example of sharing a testimony is the lame man in Acts chapter 3:1–11. He was not ashamed to praise God in the presence of others. Churches and individuals experience phases of growth. Each phase advances to another spiritual level of maturity. If a church is not being nurtured, then it can't nurture others.

What is said in this chapter is in no way the total answer for developing a viable and credible ministry of discipleship. The overall theme of the chapter has been that churches should take a more serious look at discipleship and develop their ministries in preparation for developing individuals. Not enough emphasis is stressed on the ministry of discipleship. The church is not fully experiencing their blessing. There is time for a change for the better.

There is a need to restore this needed ministry. Churches are in non-compliance and must get busy emphasizing and implementing a viable discipleship ministry in the church. Everyone is responsible to God for helping to make disciples. There are many undeveloped disciples in the church and the focus must be changed to develop healthy disciples.

The church is now in a new century and it's time for us to be about our Father's business. Jesus charged his disciples by saying, "Follow me and I will make you fishers of men"(Matthew 4:19, NKJV). A church becomes healthy through adequate training, prayer, commitment, love and dedication for the ministry of discipleship. The following essentials for nurturing a healthy church are vital for the life and growth of the church. These essentials are biblically based (John 15:1–5).

Walking by Faith

Believers must have faith. There is no way to do anything for

God and Jesus without it. "Without faith, it is impossible to please God" (Hebrews 11:4). If Christians are not walking by faith, then how are they walking? If they are walking on their own, then they will always be on edge. This means they trust themselves. When their own trust runs out, who do they turn to? When individuals walk by faith, it gives them the right to testify about the goodness of God. Having faith validates one's relationship with God. It authenticates his or her spiritual claim as Christians.

Implementing Forgiveness

Churches that take a long time to forgive are certainly unhealthy. When people refuse to forgive, they are dying spiritually and their testimony is meaningless, and when individuals have been mistreated, they are hurt, disappointed, bitter and sometimes paranoid. Their trust level for others is low. Their confidence in others is not high. They can't see the big picture because of the smoke screen. Forgiveness is a requirement and not an option. Jesus said "But if you do not forgive men their sins, your Father will not forgive your sins" (Matthew 6:15). Forgiveness is necessary for one to really live a healthy spiritual life. It is the responsibility of believers to try and rectify ill feelings as soon as possible. Unrectifed issues destroy relationships and one's spiritual life becomes marred because of unforgiveness. True disciples will seek forgiveness and will forgive those who mistreat them.

STUDY REVIEW GUIDE: THE RESULTS OF HARVEST WORK

Biblical Truth

Believers were saved to grow and develop
into Christian maturity.

Key Word

GROW: The Greek word for grow is *auxano*,
which means to increase. It is increasing for God's
church. This word means that one never stops
growing. The word is pronounced as *owx-an'-o*.

Memory Verses

1 Peter 2:1–2

Point of Emphasis

Every believer should be concerned about others
who are not growing and experiencing God.

Theological Reflection

Your theological views and reflection from this study.

Personal Application

Your thoughts on how this study has impacted you.

Study Questions

1. How important is it for Christians to grow?

2. How much do you think you can grow?

3. What are the steps for a healthy believer?

4. How does the biblical truth relate to your life?

5. What are the vital signs for growing a healthy church? Compare them.

6

True Love for the Harvest

Philippi: Being a Faithful and Loving Church

> "I thank my God every time I remember you. In all my prayers for all of you, I always pray with joy because of your partnership in the gospel from the first day until now, being confident of this, that he who began a good work in you will carry it on to completion until the day of Christ Jesus" (Philippians 1:3–6).

God is calling for faithful and loving believers. Embedded in the passion of commitment, Paul wrote this letter while he was imprisoned in Rome. This was his second Missionary Journey (Acts 16:12–40). Philippi was a Roman Colony. "Therefore loosing from Troas, we came with a straight course to Samothracia, and the next day to Neapolis; And from thence to Philippi, which is the chief city of that part of Macedonia, and a colony: and we were in that city abiding certain days" (Acts 16:11–12).

This letter was more intimate than any other letters Paul wrote. It was a real passionate and loving letter. It was a personal thank you letter for aiding him on his journey. He just could not thank the Philippians enough. He sincerely prayed for them, as they were partners with him in the gospel. Similar to the message of the Ephesians, which was written from a Roman prison, the Philippians was a true Church when it came to the teachings of Jesus Christ.

The Phillippian Church

In order to be the church that God is calling for, the Church at Philippi was a passionate church. This church was concerned about the welfare of Paul while he was on his journeys. He was under house arrest in Rome for two years. Paul did not ask for anything while he was in prison, but God provided for him. The gospel was in his heart and he wanted to share it with a faithful and loving congregation. Stott writes, "At all events, it was in this way that the gospel of God came to Philippi and created a church. It is surely no wonder that people in whom Paul saw all the supernatural powers of grace at work and for whom he had himself given so much should be as dear to him as his letter reveals."[48] Paul's intention was for the Philippian believers to keep unity. Unity in any church is an asset to believers because it helps to keep churches healthy. As a great example, the Philippian church was a healthy church.

The Philippian church has mastered the art of being disciples that God admires. They practiced what they believed. This is because joy and love were major parts of their daily involvement. They were impressive in their quest for a loving relationship with God. Mastering the art of making disciples certainly gave rise to their unity. God is always pleased with any church that endeavors to advocate the spirit of unity.

Keeping unity kept the church a loving entity in the community. For a man in prison, Paul had a vision amid all of the oppositions he faced. The letter to the Philippians has been called by two titles. It has been called the "Epistle of Excellent Things", so indeed it is, and it had been called the Epistle of Joy."[49] Regardless of what Paul experienced, he was determined to leave a positive message with the Philippians' Church. There was so much going on at that time, and joy needed to be shared.

The Letter to the Philippians

The letter to the Philippians was written when Paul was imprisoned in Rome around A.D. 62. This letter was quite different from his other letters. The tone of the letter expresses a warm invitation to want to be with people such as these. He wrote to regular people who accepted his challenge as well as his practical theology. Paul and the Philippians had a spiritual marriage and a relationship that bonded them in a way that could not be destroyed. He wrote this letter about the same time or immediately after Ephesians. This letter shares Paul's idea of a committed church in difficult and trying times. His idea of a committed church is one that prays and shows compassion. The main focus of this letter is to learn to have joy and fellowship with believers as well as joy in Jesus. Joy will be communicated more in detail latter in this chapter.

The Marks of A Discipling Church

Every church has a reputation, character and mark, whether negative or positive. This means that churches may be clueless as to what effect they may have on individuals. The marks of a church really tell what that church is all about. Regardless of what happens, the eyes of the world are on the church. It does not mean that the biblical church should have a paranoia complex, but focus on being a discipling church. Mark Denver, the author of *Nine Marks of a Healthy Church,* gives nine marks in which a church must develop believers as faithful servants:

- Expositional Preaching
- Biblical Theology
- The Gospel
- Biblical Understanding of Conversion
- Biblical Understanding of Evangelism
- Biblical Understanding of Church Membership
- Biblical Church Discipline
- Concern for Discipleship and Growth
- Biblical Church Leadership.[50]

It is my belief that a discipling church is a healthy church. They are one in the same. When the church understands the significance of taking on the marks of a discipling church, then it has submitted to God faithfully. As we come to understand our own inconsistency as Christians, it forces us to seek God more in our lives. Mark Denver hit the core with the above nine marks of a healthy Church. In the context of this book, I will share other marks in which I believe is essential for the church to remain faithful and reclaim its integrity as believers in Christ. The Philippians had certain marks as a loving and faithful church. There is a call on each of our lives, and we must live for God to fully understand, the Philippians had the following marks as a healthy church:

- A Theology of Stewardship
- A Theology of Worship
- The Recognition of Partners as Leaders
- Accepting God's plans for Leadership
- Understanding God's plan for Christian Growth
- The Faithful Believer
- Paul's Encouragement for Unity and Humility
- The Joy of Disciple-Making
- Practicing Good Christian Conduct

A Theology of Stewardship

Most Christians do not really fully understand stewardship. Do you have you a viable definition of stewardship? Do you think stewardship is only finances? In some churches, individuals have the titles as stewards. When you hear the word *steward,* biblically, it means "one who is a trustee for God." God has trusted us with His creation and we must take care of it with extreme care. We need to think like a steward and act like a steward. Stewardship is the first and most important mark of a discipling church. Stewardship serves as the foundation for the rest of the marks. It is important because it truly tells what a person is all about. If one is not a good steward, how can he or she be faithful and loving as the Philippians were?

Many churches identify stewardship with tithing. It is part of the big picture. God wants our time, talent and service. Being a good steward means to be obedient to God and all that God requires us to do. Good stewardship means to think about things in the order of priority. This means that we should know what is best for the Kingdom of God. Let's see what stewardship means biblically. Stewardship comes from the Greek word *oikonomos,* which means "manager of a household" and epitropos, which refers to a guardian. Both words are nouns. The Philippians were good stewards of money. They saw to it that Paul's financial needs were met. They managed the needs of the church and for Paul. Just as the Philippian churches looked out for the Apostle Paul, churches today of all faiths should look at the Philippians as a model of stewardship and do the same.

A Theology of Worship

A theology of worship is to recognize God the Father, God the Son, and God the Holy Spirit. This is a true mark of discipleship. God's people should have the mark of worship on their foreheads. It is a mark of obedience and contentment. This means wherever one is, worship can take place. Worship can take place without the liturgical form of structure. True worship is not timed, but is on time. When people are on one accord, the anointing of worship will come as a "mighty rushing wind." The presence of the triune Godhead must bless the worship moment. Worship is an expression that one gives to God through many ways. The Bible says,

"God is spirit, and his worshipers must worship in spirit and in truth" (John 4:24). The only way to worship is to worship sincerely. One will not feel adequate until worship has taken hold of his or her life. Many individuals and churches miss out on divine blessing when they try and force worship. Worship should be free flowing through the ministry of the Holy Spirit. The Holy Spirit must take over and take control of the sacred moment.

The Philippians were sensitive to worshipping God. They worshipped God through respect, love and devotion. This is certainly seen in their response to Paul. They were serious about their relationship with God. Worship to them was a way of life and relationship. They were obedient and their aim was to please God. They really had a way of relating to each other because God felt their commitment and dedication. The Church at Phillippi was connected to God because of their faithfulness.

Practicing Good Christian Conduct

There is no shortcut for Christian ethics. To the church at Corinth, Paul states, "But let all things be done decently and in order" (1 Corinthians 14:40). The word for decency is *euschemonos,* which means "to become well mannered." The people of God must see to it that conduct is the message for the church. This is one of the messages that Paul left with the church at Corinth. This message was not only for them, but all who had to practice good Christian conduct and humility. Paul's implementation of Christian conduct is biblical. Paul is more concerned about putting things in practice rather than just saying something. Action always speaks louder than words. Regardless of the joy he felt from the Philippians, conduct goes farther than how he felt. His real joy is in the church encouraging unity in their lives. This really gave him joy.

Church leaders today should strive to make life a life of good morality, which is good Christian conduct. Every pastor and church should not rest until Christian conduct becomes an ethical priority in the church. Parishioners in every congregation must avail themselves to every opportunity and to encourage individuals to match their conduct with their ministry. Therefore, in every church there are those who can encourage individuals to be committed to the lifestyle of good conduct. It has to be said that everyone does not have the same level of Christian conduct as others. Let us look at Philippians 1:27. Here Paul is concerned about believers acting with the greatest integrity and honesty in his absence. Conduct is a matter of the heart as well as the mind. This means that clergy and laity must merge with respect for the Body of Christ. Churches and homes can be reconciled through honesty and integrity.

When believers do not give themselves to the seriousness of good conduct, other things in the Body of Christ will be affected negatively. For this reason, it is important to improve our Christian conduct. A negative conduct can be changed through others having patience to provide ministry to those who are affected. This takes love and serious praying toward a common goal in creating an atmosphere that meets the approval of the Holy Spirit. Churches will be more positive while being obedient to the Word of God and submitting to living a life of commitment and conduct. Believers who have the mark as a negative conduct are spiritually unhealthy.

Unhealthy believers need direct care. They are in need of a divine prescription for their spiritual sickness. Sick believers can't really help the church minister and advocate good Christian conduct.

Talking about what it means to live a life of good Christian conduct is commendable. It is no good unless believers are willing to improve their Christian conduct. In Philippians 2:2 he says that joy is positive and it is important to practice joy and express a life of positive conduct, he says "make my joy complete by being like minded." Paul is saying that we must be like Christ. If we are not imitating Christ, we are not following in Christ's footsteps. It takes the power of the Holy Spirit for one to become more like Christ.

The Recognition of Partner Leaders (Philippians 1:1–3)

Paul was happy that he had a connection with the Church at Philippi. His motive was not to pump up these believers, but to recognize the art of true disciple-making. This was a joyous time for Paul and the believers in Philippi. He was comfortable because he had been in prayer for them. The apostle recognized that there were true disciples in Philippi. They were recipients of Joy from an apostle who had been abused by the leaders. Here is how Paul felt about the Philippians: "And this is my prayer: that your love may abound more and more in knowledge and depth of insight, so that you may be able to discern what is best and may be pure and blameless until the day of Christ, filled with the fruit of righteousness that comes through Jesus Christ–to the glory and praise of God" (Philippians 1:9–11). This is a true church, because Paul got their endorsement regarding being partners in the gospel, he recognizes them in verse 14 as being *courageous*. This recognition of courage distinguishes the church at Philippi from the rest of the churches he wrote.

On one occasion when Paul recognizes how the Phillippian church responded to him through financial support (4:14) he prefaced it by letting them know that they were the only church that supported him when he started out to Macedonia. In 2:12 he reminds them of their loyalty, commitment and dedication regarding their faithfulness as disciples continuing their work in his absence. This means that the church at Philippi was determined to be stars for God's kingdom, he says, "As you have always obeyed-not only in my presence but in my absence."[51] He was proud of their work as a church.

Look now as we see how Paul felt about individuals in the church at Philippi. He recognizes three individuals, who he felt had his interest, Eudoia, Syntche, and Clement (4:2–3) 'Paul pleaded with both Eudoia and Syntche to learn to work together.'[52] He was not slack when it came to recognizing individuals. He did by no means leave out Epaphroditus (2:25), who was loyal to Paul.

The church at Philippi set the standard for other churches during Paul's day, as well as churches in this millennium and times to come. Since he was treated so well his heart was touched by the unprecedented love for the cause of the gospel. The message Paul had for those who worked with him was a message of unity, hope and encouragement.

Leadership and Evangelism (Philippians 1:3–7)

Looking at this letter, we see Paul thanking God for the saints in Philippi. He certainly trusted God for their commitment.

The church at Philippi had what it took to chart the course with a plan and this was great assurance and encouragement. This church knew what they wanted to do while Paul was on tour. They were totally different from the Israelites when Moses was on Mt. Sinai (Exodus 19:3–5). The people made a golden calf, worshiped it, disrespected and disobeyed God. They were not supportive of Moses because they were into themselves and were lifted up in pride. Therefore, the Philippian church was the opposite of Israel and a great example of obedience.

Paul used the saints at Philippi along with the bishops and deacons to provide leadership. This was God's plan for leadership in the Philippian Church. The purpose of any ministry is to have adequate leadership and dedicated partners in ministry. Here is how Luke explains Paul's influence on Philippian believers: "Now a certain woman named Lydia heard us. She was a seller of purple from the city of Thyatira who worshipped God. The Lord opened her heart to heed things spoken by Paul" (Acts 16: 14, NKJV). Lydia was so excited and encouraged with Paul's ministry until she evangelized her own home. She begged Paul saying, "If you have judged me to be faithful to the Lord, come to my house and stay…" (Acts 16: 15, NKJV). This was a great influence on these believers. This influence was based on prayer. There was a girl who was possessed with the spirit of divination. Paul touched her life. Here is her response: "This girl followed Paul and us, and cried out, saying, "These men are the servants of the most High God, who proclaim to us the way of salvation" (Acts 16:17, NKJV).

God's purpose is to use ordinary people with leadership

ability to lead others to Christ. It is not always the intelligence or skills, but the willingness, fervor and commitment. Acts 16:17 really is the Great Commission in action. It was no accident that this girl followed Paul and his ministry partners; it was God's plan. This girl was demon possessed and God seized the opportunity through Paul to make a difference in her life as well as others. The church has to encourage leaders to take on the role of leading others to Christ. Furthermore, "The work of ministry begins in the recognition of all Christians; it marks the church's giving of its own life to the world."[53] Giving to the world means giving up the things of the world. Reaching lives for eternity is the divine calling given by God, and our response is obedience.

Salvation was the focus of Paul's ministry in Philippi. He desired to save them from any turmoil or disaster. He wanted them to have the assurance of being saved. Being saved is a part of discipleship. They needed to know that they could open their hearts to God and be blessed. Paul was a great example of the leadership that God had in mind for the Church at Philippi. Even from his prison cell, "About midnight Paul and Silas were praying and singing hymns to God and the other prisoners were listening to them" (Acts 16:25). It was not over with the singing and praying. Paul's and Silas' influence reached the heart of the prison keeper. He desired to change. "And he brought them out and said, "Sirs, what must I do to be saved? So they said, "Believe on the Lord Jesus Christ and you will, you and your household" (Acts 16:30–31). It does not make a difference with God regarding a person's lifestyle; it is never too late to be saved.

Part 2: The Harvest Factor

God's Plan for Spiritual Growth (Philippians 1: 8–11)

The beginning of this chapter focuses on how Paul felt about recognizing others as leaders and partners in the gospel. He now goes deeper as he really talks about how he feels about the Philippians: "God can testify how I long for all of you with the affection of Christ Jesus. And this is my prayer: that your love may abound more and more in knowledge and depth of insight" (Philippians 1:8–9). The first two verses of this chapter focuses on the leadership of the Philippian Church. Paul recognizes that nothing positive could be done apart from these leaders and disciples. He is concerned about disciples growing spiritually.

The growth of every believer depends on his or her relationship with God. This section of chapter one reveals and describes really how much faith Paul has in God. He trusts in God regarding how much affection he has for the church. He talks about "fruits of righteousness." This phrase is a phrase of being identified with God and the work of Christ. The work of Christ extends beyond our comfort zones.

Paul ends this section of chapter one with a great expression: "To the glory and praise of God" (1:11b). It is important that we today must remember to praise God in all that we do. Our spiritual growth is connected to giving God glory and praising him.

There are five chapters in Philippians. Chapter one deals with a theology of love in that Paul looked at his own preaching and personal circumstances, but yet he expressed loved in a high fashion. This chapter is the foundation chapter, which begins with a divine salutation recognizing Paul and Timothy as servants of Christ, who is the head.

Chapters one through five apply to every Christian and how the application of the theology of Love must be evident in each believer's life. Chapter two is about humility. Chapter three is about the knowledge of Christ and chapter four, the presence of Christ. In this ministry to the church at Philippi, Paul was thankful to the Philippians for their love and compassion." I can do all things through Christ who strengthens me. Nevertheless, you have done well that you shared in my distress" (Philippians 4:13–14, NKJV).

The Church's Faithfulness

The church must remain faithful by helping other Christians as Jesus demonstrated in Matthew. Regardless of how the Philippian church acted in Paul's absence, they still had joy. They thought that the gospel was not going to be preached since Paul was imprisoned. Paul shares what it means to be around a faithful and loving church. He was well pleased about the love and joy he received from the church at Philippi. The entire church at Philippi had to have had a better understanding of faithfulness. This faithfulness is associated with unity because there had been some problems with disunity (4:1–3). Paul knew that disunity would destroy the congregation. He really encouraged them to practice living in unity. Living in unity is a sure sign of faithfulness. If any church remains faithful, then it is the discipling church that God is looking for in these days. Those churches that are not faithful need to take a closer look at its discipleship and how best the church can foster unity.

Every spiritual leader would do good to take a look at Paul regarding encouraging congregational unity. Congregational unity builds a stronger congregational life. He also reminded them that Christ was still in charge. What was important was to follow the leadership of Christ and to practice humility as well.

Paul's Encouragement for Unity and Humility (1:27–2:11)

Paul was able to see firsthand that the church at Philippi makes unity and humility a major part of their personality. His encouragement to them was to look to the future and stay together as a church should. He meant that nothing could be done with disunity at the core of existence. It was impossible to love without unity, properly forgive and even worship God. Paul used Jesus as the prime example of humility (2:5–6). Humility is the key to the doorway of Christ's blessings. His focus for them was that Christ was and is the central focus of being together. The church could not and will not prosper with inner rivalry among believers. What Paul was saying was that the church could not afford to risk its health (spiritual growth) by disregarding unity and humility.

The Joy of Disciple-Making

Basically, Church leaders and parishioners have not really expressed their discipleship through joy. To have joy is to have love. They both go hand-in-hand. However, many churches and church organizations have put a premium on self and the organization, causing dissensions. I have found that many in churches and church groups do not seem to have joy. They claim joy during worship, but when the rubber hits the road and the cookie crumbles, the real answer comes out. Because of this, the evidence of joy is not there. Personally, without having joy, one can and will become spiritually morbid. If one is morbid, one is sour and this is no way to leave an impression of disciple-making.

There is a song which says, "This joy I have the world didn't give it to me, and the world can't take it away." This is a true song. Many may sing it but may not have relevance in their life. Joy is the key in Philippians. It is the word of the hour. Everything that Paul did, he did it with joy. This is the only letter he wrote with anticipated excitement.

In most traditional churches, expressing joy through worship could be more evident. This means that there are individuals who display joy differently, meaning they are less charismatic than others. Some people express joy quietly and others more lurid. The church has to disciple with joy from both sides. This is because there are different people who express God differently. In essence, there are those who prefer to work with those who are emotional rather than those who are less emotional. This means that there is a need to minister diversely. Diversity makes up the disciple-making church.

I used to sell life insurance in the South for many years, collecting premiums weekly and monthly. I had one client on my debit (collecting route) that every time I saw her, she was full of joy! As a matter of fact, she greeted me with a warm smile. She shared with me positively when many times I was a little down. She loved the Lord and did not mind expressing joy. She was the epitome of a joyous saint who really loved the Lord. Christ was her conversation, and she was not bashful in expressing her feelings. When I left her presence, I was encouraged to meet others with the same joy she shared with me. The modern day church really needs to have joyful saints just like the person mentioned above. There are many disciple-making churches that need to raise the level of joy in their church. They should share joy and use the joy of the Holy Spirit more often. One will not and cannot experience the love of God without complete joy in his or her life.

As an example, when Paul talked about joy, he used words and or phrases such as: "Rejoice in the Lord always" (4:4), "I rejoiced greatly" (4:10), and "I am glad and rejoice with all of you" (2:17). Christ did not leave his church joyless. The Bible says, "Abide in me and I in you" (John 15:4, NKJV). The word *abide* comes from the Greek word *meno*, which means to become stationary in Christ. Paul confirms that the church at Corinth needed to have joy in their lives. The Apostle James as well as Peter refers to the word *joy*.

Therefore, the discipling church must have a strong foundation regarding biblical and theological positions. Paul encouraged the Philippian congregation to develop a trusting theology, meaning that God will take care of your needs (4:19–20). He spoke these words with a sure sense of conviction. This was related to his faith in God and believing that God would take care of him through the Philippians, that's why he had joy, and his joy was in the Lord.

It has been traditionally known that most churches that express joy were associated with Charismatic churches. Charismatic churches were considered churches that were highly emotional. Charismatic comes from the Greek word *charisma*, mostly associated with gifts. In a way, joy is connected to gifts. The believer must use his or her gift when serving others and serving must be done with joy.

A Theology of Salvation

The Apostle Paul's stance on salvation is a major point of his theology. It is evident that those who have not yet looked at Jesus as the example has the opportunity to do so. Paul makes this biblical claim by saying, "Therefore, my beloved, as you have obeyed, so now not only as in my presence but much more in my absence, work out your own salvation with fear and trembling" (Philippians 2:12, NKJV). Jesus died in order that one can be saved. What does Paul mean by working out salvation? The verb *work* in the Greek is what Paul says regarding the need to be completely obedient to God. One must put Christ first and totally trust Him as well as have extreme respect for Him.

Just as in Paul's day, we in the twenty-first century must remember that salvation is the major part of discipling lives. People have the opportunity to help others regardless of their theological or philosophical purity to be able to put aside such position and take a stronger look at the message of salvation. From personal experience, I find that many individuals have not taken their salvation seriously. They in fact make a valid claim to personal salvation while living in bitterness and even unforgiveness. Serving in any church where strife is eminent leaves very little room for authentic discipleship.

Paul exhorts believers to "do all things without grumbling or questioning, that you be blameless and innocent, children without blemish in the midst of a crooked and perverse generation among whom you shine as lights in the world" (Philippians 2:14–15, NKJV). This should be a challenge to every believer to reflect, rethink and reevaluate his or her personal relationship with Christ. Personal reflection is connected to the goal of making disciples. I have experienced that many disciples are less concerned about making disciples because they have not learned the art. Those who are not in the network of discipleship tend to do other things in the church to substitute for what they are not doing. When this happens, it is pure negligence. Even in a divided or grumbling church, there is a need for immediate support to those who are serious. Those who are not serious need encouragement.

There are those in churches who are blessed to have people work together to advocate the art of disciple-making positively. They overlook the small talk, grand pettiness and pride. People, regardless of their position in the church, must refuse to listen to negative remarks that impede the ministry of the church. Therefore, those who are in leadership positions must think more of their relationship with Christ rather than their position in the church. Positions have a tendency to escalate pride but a Christ centered relationship deflates positions and pride.

God's Purpose for Believers

There are many individuals who are clueless when it comes to God's purpose in their life. Paul affirms, "For it is God who works in you to will and to act according to his good purpose" (Philippians 2:13). Each believer has the opportunity to be like Christ. In this context, God's purpose is for every believer to act like he or she belongs to Christ. This means that we do not get involved in trivial matters. Again in Philippians 2:14, he refers in another way to conduct. He says, "Do everything without complaining or arguing, so that you may become blameless and pure, children of God without fault in a crooked and depraved generation, in which you shine like stars in the universe."

God's purpose for believers is that we shine as stars. Jesus says, "Let your light shine before men, that they may see your good deeds and praise your Father in heaven" (Matthew 5:16). God intends for the world to see Him through the believer. Therefore, we have to represent God in the light and not the dark. There are too many individuals trying to glow in the dark when the light is not in them. This does not help nor reflect church health. God wants us to shine in three ways: (1) prayer (2) the Word (3) and faith. If we shine in with prayer, the word and faith, the world can and will see us. Believers are not to be seen for personal gratification, but for the glory of God. We are stars because every believer disciple has a part and that part must make its impact in the Body of Christ. Believers work together synergistically, but when we are apart, we have our own tailor-made ministry.

The Problem of the Flesh

The third chapter of Philippians starts with the reiteration that there is danger in submitting to the flesh because our focus is to worship God. Paul was trying to encourage the saints to stay away from those who mean you no good. Paul refers to them as "dogs" (3:2). Dog here is not literally a puppy, but is metaphorical of moral impurity. When anyone's character is as low as a dog, it displeases God. Unhealthy believers are caught up in moral impurity. They can so easily get caught up in the flesh. Flesh here is *Sarx,* which means the unregenerate state of individuals, or mere sinful nature. The flesh is a true sign of an unhealthy believer. When the flesh attacks the believer, and the believer submits to the flesh, it leaves an unhealthy life.

The flesh will destroy positive intentions if it gets too deep into one's spirit. The flesh is the challenging opponent from hell. To disregard the flesh means do not allow it to set up rule in your life. One needs the guidance of the Holy Spirit to effectively conquer the flesh. It takes faith to be able to overlook the sadistic and vile motives of the flesh. Believers must constantly and daily strive for a healthy relationship with God.

Too many in the church operate in the flesh and that is the major reason why ministry is impeded. The things we have not done for Christ can never be made up. Time wasted is time lost. Those things that seemed to be right were not. From experience, Paul did not want the Philippians to make the same mistake that he made. "But whatever was to my profit I now consider loss for the sake of Christ" (Philippians, 3:7). There is a need to take a close look at how Paul wasted time while doing things that were of no avail. He had his own agenda and his own righteousness.

At one time, Paul was not on the same page with Christ. He made the point regarding his own ignorance. He acknowledges this by saying: "What is more, I consider everything a loss compared to the surpassing greatness of knowing Christ Jesus my Lord, for whose sake I have lost all things. I consider them rubbish, that I may gain Christ" (3:8). He had to put things in priority. He had to totally submit to Christ. Things had changed for Paul and he desired to change his course and direction regarding his relationship with Christ.

A Commitment to Know God

In Philippians 3:10, he states that the process of getting to know Christ is self evaluation. "I want to know Christ and the power of his resurrection and the fellowship of sharing in his sufferings, becoming like him in his death." One must do his or her own theological reflection as he or she matures in the faith. It is impossible to do ministry and not know the one who came to minister to us. Knowing God is a daily process. God is looking for each believer to get to know Him. To be an effective and successful believer, one must not rest until he or she comes to know God. Knowing Christ means that a relationship exists. To know God is to have a personal relationship with Him as we seek to understand His attributes.

Our thirst to know Him will lead us to develop a healthy and lasting relationship. Some of His attributes are love, mercy, justice, immutability and omniscience. In striving to know God, Paul is really talking about a higher calling when he says, "Not that I have already obtained all this, or have already been made perfect, but I press on to take hold of that for which Christ Jesus took hold of me" (Philippians 3:12). The leadership of the church must know Him in order to encourage others to know Him. There is only so much we can know about God. Therefore, we should know that we know about God well enough to experience God.

A Commitment to Stand Fast in the Lord

The fourth chapter starts with an exhortation for believers to stand fast in the Lord. This is a chapter of faith and confidence. Paul here passionately desired to encourage the Philippians to stand fast in the Lord. He refers to them as "dearly beloved" (Philippians 4:1, KJV). This implies a relationship of love. There are too many believers without the faith to stay the course. God allows us to experience many circumstances which are designed to make us stronger. The Holy Spirit is there to comfort us and encourage us when the fuel of fire has dwindled down. Many have given up because of a lack of faith and a lack of fuel. Fuel here is the anointing from the Holy Spirit. Contentment affirms Paul's faith in God. He is straightforward when it comes to his belief.

True Contentment

Faith is mentioned 14 times in the New Testament. Philippians 4:11 specifically speaks of Paul's faith in which he confirms "for I have learned, in whatsoever state I am, therewith to be content." Paul was completely satisfied because of the many adversities in his life. He was experienced, and if anyone could tell us anything, Paul could. A disciple must rest assured that God shares in our contentment. Being content says one has no doubts. This is the acceptance of the will of God.

How can one know that he or she is content and how different it is from non-Christians? The Bible gives the evidence that believers are in God's hand. The Bible teaches to "Keep your lives free from the love of money and be content with what you have, because God has said, "Never will I leave you; never will I forsake you" (Hebrews 13:5). God has promised us in His word that we are to be faithful and live by faith. Having faith is the major difference between a believer and a non-believer.

There are three qualities in Philippians 4:12–14, 19 which give a description of the contented believer:

Knowledge Knowing is not being ashamed to tell others what you know. How we use our knowledge determines our destiny. We must learn how to accept knowledge when there is a need. This is true contentment. Knowledge is knowing the secret of being content. In life, contentment comes through knowing and understanding God's direction.

Dealing with Suffering It sounds ironic to imply or say that a Christian is content with suffering. There are different views concerning suffering in the life of a believer. Some feel that suffering is punishment for sin or wrongdoing. As a believer, whether one sins or not, suffering comes with the territory. Jesus suffered for us. Why should believers be free from suffering? Some theologians believe that if believers buy into the idea that suffering is part of the Christian experience, they feel that is bad theology. A contented believer knows how to look over demeaning circumstances and move on. The person who is content has a testimony to tell, a prayer to pray and a commitment to keep. Being contented with God is far more than a false sense of contentment with the world. With non-believers a false sense of contentment will not last because it is not contentment with God.

Total Trust This is the chance to really step out on faith and see the hand of God working in your life. God has given us what we need to trust Him. Trusting in God is declaring that whatever needs to be done it will. Contentment is tough during trial, but with faith, one can stand the test.

The contented disciple has all three qualities in Philippians, 4:12–14, 19. The disciple that is contented will give his or her total life to Christ amid problems and circumstances. If one is not content, there will be consequences that can cause a spiritual setback. One cannot serve while being burdened. The disciple must be humble to serve and willing to learn.

Christians must do their best to be consistent in implementing the above qualities. They must take being content a step further. There are three additional key qualities for contentment: (1) give God the glory, (2) salute every saint (3) and the closing blessing of the grace of God. We must always wish God's blessings on the saints. If one is not content, then he or she will not implement the above qualities. Jesus desired for his followers to be content and that it should affect the ministry of Paul, the Ephesians and the church at Philippi.

Contentment is clearly outlined in Acts 20:24 when Paul gave his farewell message to the Ephesian elders. It should be a concerted effort that the church today remains faithful, loving and healthy. When I say the church, I am referring to the Body of Christ and not just one local church.

STUDY REVIEW GUIDE: TRUE LOVE FOR THE HARVEST

Biblical Truth

The work that we do is the work that God has in us.

Key Word

STEWARDSHIP: The Greek word for a steward is *oikonomos* (the word is pronounced with an h (hoikonomos), which means a house servant.

Memory Verse

Philipians 3:12

Point of Emphasis

Pleasing God is a full-time commitment of love.

Theological Reflection

Your theological views and reflection from this study.

Personal Application

Your thoughts on how this study has impacted you.

Study Questions

1. What are your views of the church at Philippi?

2. What is the difference between the Church at Philippi and the other churches Paul ministered to?

3. Are there any similarities between the Church at Philippi and your church today, and or the Body of Christ?

4. How does the biblical truth relate to your ministry?

5. How do you think you would have responded to Paul's need if you were living in his day?

THE POWER FACTOR

In this section of the book, the power factor is the gauge that reads the temperature of the work of the church. It is the reason for being and doing what has to be done. A powerless church is a church that is full of problems and has a spiritual deficit. Churches need to avoid the spiritual deficit. The church must use its power under the anointing of the Holy Spirit. The church cannot engage in spiritual warfare, nor be able to stand without power. I must adamantly say that there is a lack of prayer in many churches, African Americans, multi-cultural, non-denominational, Asians, Euro Americans and many others. There is a need to reclaim the total ministry of discipleship and do the real business of the Lord. Every believer needs the leading of the Holy Spirit to be able to be genuine and faithful followers of Christ. Also we cannot sit by and remain silent regarding social justice issues in America as well as the world.

THE CHURCH UTILIZING POWER THROUGH CONFLICT

ENGAGING IN SPIRITUAL WARFARE

> "For our struggle is not against flesh and blood, but against the rulers, against the authorities, against the powers of this dark world and against the spiritual forces of evil in the heavenly realms" (Ephesians 6:12).

Spiritual warfare is an ongoing battle.

In every phase of life, there is a need for deliverance from the heavy burden of the battle of spiritual warfare. The Apostle Paul emphatically says, "For the weapons of our warfare are not carnal, but mighty in God for pulling down strongholds" (2 Corinthians 10:4, NKJV). There are three words in this verse which stand out, "weapons," "warfare" and "carnal." These terms express the theme of spiritual warfare. Spiritual warfare is a constant sadistic attack by demonic forces. The weapons we have are spiritual weapons. Spiritual weapons are the only way that believers can effectively and truthfully conquer spiritual warfare. Warfare is a constant battle between the believer and the devil. The church must be ready for this battle daily. The Bible says, "Who shall separate us from the love of Christ? Shall trouble or hardship or persecution or famine or nakedness or danger or sword? As it is written: "For your sake we face death all day long; we are considered as sheep to be slaughtered" (Romans 8:35–36). These verses sound like a military battle, but it is the battle of evil against spiritual.

Our understanding of warfare is connected with the word *stronghold.* Jesus certainly dealt with strongholds during his ministry. He was able to defeat Satan after he had fasted for forty days and forty nights (Matthew 4:2). This stronghold did not have a hold on his life and ministry. If we don't see the connection of Jesus' ministry to the battle of strongholds, we are not going to be able to stand.

Paul uses the word stronghold to raise our awareness of what is at center stage in the life of disciples. The word "stronghold" is taken from the Greek word *ochuroma,* which refers to a fortress and to make firm. It is used metaphorically in (2 Corinthians 10:4) to mean that those things we as humans encounter attack our confidence, intellect and spirit. Regardless of the stronghold, Christians must continue to walk by faith.

There has been much talk on spiritual warfare within the Body of Christ. To be more specific, the local church, families, conventions and even denominations are caught in the thicket of warfare. There are too many spiritual political strongholds in conventions and associations. Some talk about it more than others. Others only refer to it when their family or someone close to them is attacked. There are some who perhaps don't really know when spiritual warfare is present.

The church must bring its spiritual lens closer to the forefront and help prepare individuals and families to get ready and stay ready for battle. Focus must be on the ministry of the Holy Spirit. It is unfortunate that the church has been mostly silent on the issue of spiritual warfare, the same as end times prophesy. If it does not apply, they don't bother. Warfare is in the Word; it is the *Logos,* the teachings of Christ. There is much that can be shared on the subject of warfare across this country. These teachings are done by many denominations and non-denominations. Church parishioners can become involved in many activities to learn how to handle spiritual warfare, and some activities are:

- Prayer Warriors Conferences…
- End Times Conferences…
- Warfare Workshops…
- Spiritual Growth Seminars…
- Church Wide Retreats…
- Marriage Couples Retreats…
- Purpose Driven Life Conferences…
- Congregational Transformational Seminars…
- Discipleship Seminars…
- Mission Conferences…

One can choose from this list and make a decision regarding his or her own spiritual destiny. It is helpful to browse through the bookstores, Internet and find other material on the subject. The wider the spectrum of information, the better-informed individuals will be. This information should be used to know how to interact with the forces of evil. It is important that churches inform parishioners and make available resources for immediate use. I would suggest that churches even have several books and other resources in a library for quick use.

The Fight Is On

When we refer to warfare, we refer to a fight. The word warfare comes from the Greek word, *strateia,* which means strategy. Our strategy is to be ready for both defense and offense. We can't conquer without knowing how to use the weapons; therefore, it is important to have a plan for putting up a strong defense against Satan. We must use as much defense as offense. We must be clever with our offense. We must be aware that the fight is on in and outside of the church. Satan has an army to fight in the church and one to fight outside the church. The purpose is the same. The one who heads up the army in the church is the Spirit of Jezebel. In the Old Testament, Jezebel fought against the prophets of God. Therefore the Spirit of Jezebel is deep seated in the church. Jezebel is smart, deceitful, and persuasive. She has deception down to an art. Jezebel recruits and trains weak believers to rebel and fight against God's program. The "Spirit of Jezebel" is in worldly affairs, but probably not as cunning as the spirit in the church. She knows she has those in the world and does not have to be as persuasive, but is still persistent. From the world Jezebel sends her vile spirit in the church to take up residence to invade the minds and infiltrate the hearts of innocent believers, changing their path and purpose in life. That is why churches have a hard time getting ministry across to believers; it is rejected because Jezebel is being followed instead of Jesus.

Many believers are losing the battle of this warfare because they are not equipped to use the weapons of warfare. Just as the military trains every soldier before battle, the church must do the same with disciples. Young disciples can't go out to witness and share the gospel without the proper training, weapons and clothing. Believers can't be intimidated by the evil strategy of Satan. I mentioned the importance of training in chapters one and two. Satan, the deceiver, is always on the offense. This is the direct attack because many times we are not on guard.

Our weapons are really found in Ephesians 6:13–18. The writer of Ephesians has outlined the weapons of our warfare. God has given us seven weapons of warfare: *truth, breastplate of righteousness, feet of peace, the shield of faith, the helmet of salvation, the sword of the Spirit, and prayer.* These seven weapons of warfare are the perfect number for God's protection in our lives. The sword of the Spirit is the only offensive weapon mentioned, and the rest are defensive weapons. This is because we protect ourselves with the sword. We are in need of every one of these weapons, and if we don't have them, we will soon fall prey to the adversary.

I will for clarity explain some Greek words for wickedness. This is in no way an exhaustive study on the word wickedness. There are other synonyms in scripture that refer to wickedness, such as malice, maliciousness, and naughtiness.

However, for this study it is only a bird's eye view into the nature of the meaning of how wickedness is used in scripture. *Spiritual warfare is a term taken from the following words: wickedness, wicked, evil and iniquity.* Wickedness comes from the following Greek Words: *poneria, poneros, athesmos and kakia.* Kakia is a noun, which is used to explain evil. The war of spiritual warfare has been declared on every believer, and every believer must be prepared to defend against such opposition.

Subsequently, every new believer must receive basic training before going on the battlefield. After basic training, Christians must go through advanced training before going to combat. When I was in the army, I took basic training and advanced training. After advanced training I was ready for battle. Later I was shipped overseas for that purpose. I did not do much fighting, but I was prepared just in case.

Spiritual warfare is a direct attack against the Body of Christ. This is what it does. This is the primary objective of spiritual warfare. It is an attack because Satan does not desire for the church to survive. What is spiritual warfare? How is the believer handling this attack? These are very important questions. Spiritual warfare means to drain the fruit, fervor and power of the believer, causing spiritual deformity. When spiritual warfare has lifted up its ugly head, the church is engaged in combat. Combat is when two opposing forces intend to defeat each other. One will win and one will lose, unless a peace treaty is signed, in this case the devil refuses to accept peace. The prevailing winner is prepared mentally and emotionally. When soldiers go to battle, they must be physically, mentally, emotionally and spiritually prepared for battle. Before going to combat, adequate training is the necessary factor. Soldiers are trained to succeed and not surrender. If captured, do not comprise but be brave and not bashful.

Just as soldiers go to combat, the Christian is ever engaged in spiritual warfare, which is spiritual combat. Just as the military, believers are trained to survive and not surrender. If they are captured, do not comprise, but be brave and not bashful. I cannot say it enough: the church must have a reliable discipleship training program in place before disciples go on the battlefield. Before Jesus commissioned His disciples, He met with them and trained them for the total mission and ministry of the church. "And as He walked by the Sea of Galilee, He saw Simon and Andrew his brother casting a net into the sea; for they were fishermen. Then Jesus said to them, Come after me, and I will make you become fishers of men" (Mark 1: 16–17, NKJV). Jesus said "He would make them become fishers of men." Make means to train, and teach. Make comes from the same Greek word as used in Matthew 28:19.

This ever-engaging battle of spiritual warfare can take a toll on our lives if we don't have faith. Burdens are everywhere, battles are everywhere and disappointments are everywhere. Faith is the answer to our strong offense. The Christians and non-Christians are wrestling with oppositions from the president of hell, which is Satan. The non-Christian does not know how to deal with these battles. Christians are anticipating the day when we will be set free from our setbacks. There is a great wrestling match going on between Satan and the church. We wrestle day and night. Jesus and his disciples wrestled with the conventional wisdom in His day. Our answer, Christians and non-Christians, lies in Jesus

Christ. In order to be delivered, the church must use wisdom and tactfulness. Jesus gave His disciples a lecture on human interaction. He said "Behold, I send you forth as sheep in the midst of wolves: be ye wise as serpents and harmless as doves" (Matthew 10:16, KJV). It is not good for one to go with the wrong attitude, for there will be danger at hand. The progress of the church has been impeded because many have been held captive at the hand of spiritual warfare.

Reclaiming the Missing in Action

In many churches, as a result of warfare, there are individuals who are missing in action. They are either spiritually dead or prisoners of war. When I say war, I am referring to spiritual warfare. Warfare is designed to discredit our testimony and witness. Therefore, Satan has seduced and captured a great number of members who are very weak in the faith. They were captured because they could not protect themselves and did not know how to stay out of the sight of the enemy during intense battle. Jesus had one of His disciples missing in action. Judas was missing when he betrayed Jesus. He was mentality captured by the authorities in his day. Judas' mind was not on Christ; his mind was to satisfy those who wanted Jesus.

There are several reasons why some of the disciples today are missing in action. (1) They are missing because they went out on the battlefield unprepared. They could not fight and they could not see, because they did not take any oil in their lamps like five of the ten virgins as recorded in Matthew twenty-five. (2) The second reason is that they were weak in biblical and theological foundations. Studying and applying God's Word has not been for some a priority. However, when people are weak, they are not able to effectively fight the spiritual battle. This is because "This is a battle unto death. We must come under strict discipline of body, mind, and spirit. There is no place in this service for the double minded or the sluggard. Only those who are crucified with Christ will know the victory that overcomes the world."[54] Those who have first hand experience on the battlefield are well prepared to encourage others and to convince them that the only way to survive is to have faith.

Warfare and the Old Testament

It would not be complete to undertake a study of spiritual warfare without a historical biblical look at the Old Testament. The idea of spiritual warfare comes from the core of Satan's presence. Warfare is a direct attack against the divine principles and plan of God. Even in heaven, spiritual warfare started with Lucifer, who wanted to take over heaven. As a result, God threw him out along with his hosts of angels. I will mention a small number of instances regarding warfare in the Old Testament. The first instance of warfare is found in Genesis. God instructed Adam not to eat of the tree in the midst of the garden. Wickedness entered the mind of Eve and persuaded her to eat and tempted Adam to do the same. This was spiritual wickedness.

Adam and Eve's conscience alerted them that something had happened. They realized they were naked. Wickedness will allow you to see your nakedness, your shamefulness and your disobedience. Nakedness is when your spirituality has been punctured by the very presence and power of sin. Ever since that happened, humanity has been in the need of redemption. Since wickedness has invaded the human family, it has left an indelible mark of unrighteousness on the human conscious.

As we know it, "Cain killed Abel." This killing was out of pure jealousy. Jealousness can destroy relationships. Those who are disciples must not allow jealousness to ruin their spiritual lives. Those who lived during Old Testament times and proclaimed allegiance to God were faithful. As stated earlier in chapter one, we know that a disciple is a follower and a learner of Christ. Those in the Old Testament who walked by faith, their lives served as a foundation for believing in God.

Warfare did not stop there, it caught a wave of wickedness and moved ashore to many Old Testament characters such as: Joshua and the Battle of Jericho, David and Bathsheba, and Saul and Jonathan. These are all examples of having experienced spiritual warfare. Spiritual warfare attacked them in every facet of their involvement. Joshua had his hands full with the Battle of Jericho. David had an intense obsession for Bathsheba; the evilness of warfare was directing and leading him to commit murder and adultery. Saul experienced an evil spirit. His motive was to do wrong. Jonathan's life was threatened, all because of the nature of evil. Wickedness followed them with a passion. There were many kings in the Old Testament who were wicked. King Zedekiah was a wicked king. King Nebuchadnezzar was wicked. These kings did not have God on their agenda.

The main idea of this section is warfare and not discipleship. The purpose is to show how warfare attacked those in the Old Testament who walked with God by faith. Let us take a look at how God used David in a specific situation. Young

David walked with God, and God protected him and caused him to defeat Goliath. Goliath waged war against the Israelites (2 Samuel. 17:4–11). This waging of war was designed to put fear in Israel. Again, this fear was the work of Satan using Goliath to destroy Israel. Regardless of what Goliath's plans were, God had another plan to defeat him in front of all of the Philistines and the Israelites. "The devil wants to take you captive and destroy you with the same tools that Goliath used against the Israelites. He wants to ruin your effectiveness with mere suggestions and lying allegations."[55] When one walks with God and obeys God, God will fight on your behalf. God's fight is not a fight based on merit, but a fight based on obedience and faithfulness.

Warfare and the Early Church

The Early Church really began with the birth of Jesus, but it was not fully recognized or manifested until after the first century Jews had heard the Gospel and then it spread. "God had prepared the way so that the disciples, after receiving the power of the Holy Spirit, could be witnesses in Jerusalem and in all Judea and Samaria and to the end of the earth" (Acts 1:8).[56] The Early Church was no exception to the infectious bitterness of wickedness and vile actions by Satan. The apostles as well as the church were confronted and focused on warfare. Bringing Satan's kingdom down during the Early Church was a challenge for the apostles. Winning over Satan's kingdom required casting out demons.

Warfare during the Early Church was significantly about being able to cast out demons. During the ministry of Peter, believers were added to the church because of the faith and belief of Peter. Their addition to the church was an asset to the battle of warfare.

> And believers were increasingly added to the Lord, multitudes of both men and women, so that they brought the sick out into the streets and laid them on beds and couches, that at least the shadow of Peter passing by might fall on them. Also a multitude gathered from the surrounding cities to Jerusalem, bringing sick people, and those who were tormented by unclean spirits, and they were all healed. (Acts 5:14–16)[57]

This act of faith and fortitude solidifies the work of the Holy Spirit. Every work of faith is grounded in the Holy Spirit. The people believed and the apostles performed. Demons were cast out and people were healed. After Peter and the apostles cast out demons, they were incarcerated (Acts 5:18). After they were put in prison, God opened the doors through the angel (Acts 5:19). There is always victory when God is in the picture and plan of warfare. We cannot bring down strongholds when we are part of the problem. Bringing down strongholds will be expanded on more later in this writing.

It must not be forgotten regarding the occasion when Phillip went to the city of Samaria and preached Christ. As a result, multitudes heeded what was spoken and unclean spirits cried out and those who were possessed and paralyzed were healed (Acts 8:5–7). This incident of warfare and casting out demons gained much attention. There was a Jew named Simon who at one time practiced sorcery and fooled the people that he believed God who later believed and was baptized and worked with Phillip (Acts 8:9, 13). After Simon believed, he thought he could buy the Holy Spirit (Acts 8: 17–18). Phillip urged him to repent of the demon of bitterness and iniquity and be forgiven by God (Acts 8: 22). Satan uses all kinds of sadistic methods and tricks to attack the church. Simon was rather eccentric in his quest for God. He had the wrong reason for the right decision. Christians need to study more on warfare because Satan and his hosts are all over. They are everywhere because "Satan appoints ruling spirits or strongholds over every principality or control area."[58] These ruling spirits represent Satan and intend to attack the Body of Christ, therefore, weakening its power to witness.

Warfare and the Present Day Disciple

The present day disciple has to experience the constant interruption and battle of demonic spirits. They are in the church, the home and the individual. Warfare is heavy in the local church and the Body of Christ. The main reason why the church has a hard time winning and influencing the nonbeliever is because the church has taken on the mentality of Jezebel and Ahab. Jezebel is still killing prophets. The mind of prophets is attacked. These spirits are in the communities in which we live, our homes, and churches! Yes churches! We are living in such a modern day society, and demons have become modern as well. However, some may still be living in the Stone Age, and they have learned how to adapt to these times. They still know how and when to attack. Demon spirits are all around wherever we go.

Christians should be able to recognize demons as entering in our territory. When they enter, they are invading unauthorized territory. They have no right to be there. Demons want to invade the Christian's territory in order to recruit new blood and those who are matured in Christ. They don't care who they get because that is their mission. Disciples today are confronted with an immeasurable amount of attacks. These attacks are represented from all walks of life, blue collar and white collar, young or old and from every culture and ethnic group. Evil spirits control this battle of the present day warfare. Evil spirits really take possession of individuals (Luke 4:33, 8:28, 16:9 and Mark 9:17). It is only those individuals who are not saved who are possessed by evil spirits.

To be possessed by a demon is to be under total control of the demon. Being controlled by the demon means they own you. In the Greek, the word "*daimonizomai*," which is a verb, is translated to mean possessed. After having been possessed, the demon influences the life of the person to act at Satan's command. This possession causes one to have true allegiance to the demonic nature of Satan.

True Christians are not possessed with an evil spirit, but with the Holy Spirit. Jesus left his disciples to do the work of casting out demons. In Mark 9:17- 23, Jesus left his disciples in charge with a boy who had been possessed. The disciples could not handle the assignment. They could not do it because they were not prayed up. They did not have on, as was said earlier, weapons of warfare. Nothing really happened until Jesus came. This young man was possessed for life until Jesus broke the bonds of evil possession and released Him to a life of peace and righteousness.

Demons come and attack in all manner of ways. They use different tactics to manipulate and annihilate. These tactics are based on how an individual interacts with Satan. Demons can enter a person by way of an unclean spirit:

> "Then they came to the other side of the sea, to the country of the Gadarenes. And when He had come out of the boat, immediately there met him a man with and unclean spirit, who had his dwelling among the tombs; and no one could bind him, not even with chains, because he had often been bound with shackles and chains, and the chains had been pulled apart by him, and the shackles had been broken in pieces, neither could anyone tame him. (Mark 5: 1–4, NKJV)[59]

The word unclean in this verse comes from the Greek word, *akathartos* which is an adjective, it means impure. The word *akathartos* modifies the noun spirit. So therefore, a person possessed with an unclean spirit is at another level of demonic possession. Uncleanness carries a foul odor of evilness. This unclean and foul smell is an odor of the mind, heart and attitude. It goes without saying that Satan is dirty and foul. Disciples of Christ need to keep clean and not be influenced by Satan. This means that we can't mingle with Satan and expect God to use us for His Glory.

Day to Day Conflicts

Demons do not care who they oppose. They plan hard and always think how they are going to do what is at hand. In another sense, conflicts are forms of warfare. It is the plan of the enemy. Because of these day-to-day conflicts, they are in the church and the family. Let us begin with the latter first.

The family is a prime target in these days as well as days of old. They are a target because there is a vast amount of interaction among family members. These conflicts do not start at adulthood, but during childhood. The evil spirits will use the most innocent child to start a major storm to destroy a family. That is why it is important for the entire family to be covered in the blood of Jesus. When we are covered in the blood, it means to know without a doubt that divine protection is in our lives. It is reclaiming our experience with our Savior. The main reason why evil spirits leech onto children, is because they have not grown into spiritual maturity. However, there are some adults who have not grown spiritually as well. In this case, evil spirits will find the weakest spot in childhood as well as adulthood.

Many families are attacked when it is time to go to church, regardless of the day of the week. An argument can start from the most trivial matter, which mushrooms and looms into a gruesome argument. These types of circumstances are designed by the evil one to distract individuals from continuing in a discipleship mode. It has been said, "Every family has a black sheep." This means that that person is prone to causing trouble or embarrassing family members or self. Subsequently, they may admit or accept the embarrassment. There are family members in every family who try hard to walk with Jesus. Walking with Jesus is a statement of faith. This means that those individuals are disciples of Jesus. It becomes a greater conflict when their faith is tried. Regardless of these conflicts, the struggle goes on.

The family has to deal with those in their family who are involved in drugs, alcohol, thievery, spousal abuse, unemployment, infidelity and even murder. With these issues and problems, each family will need counseling. These circumstances cause conflicts and at some point, someone becomes depressed and devastated.

The church can be a link between the family and the community to provide support regarding such conflicts. These conflicts in the family will definitely spread to the church, and sometimes what is private becomes public. What's private becoming public is sometimes caused by leaky lips, from both family members and sometimes the leadership of the church. This is when the church has to draw the line and provide security and support to families.

Let me share a story that I wrote for a high school reading class I taught in Florida: Mr. Amber is very haughty because he walks around thinking he is better than anyone else. He and his friends conjured up stories about several neighbors to discredit their character. Many of the neighbors did not want to start trouble, so they ignored them. However, one of the neighbors retaliated by throwing eggs on Mr. Amber and his friends' cars. Mr. Amber is the ringleader because he is so obsessed with telling lies. He has a hard time refraining from telling lies. On several occasions, Mrs. Amber has provoked Mr. Amber. However, he mistreated her at home because he is so obsessed with telling lies and he can't control his anger. She caught him telling lies and he became very displeased. He then kicked down the door and knocked out the window.

Mrs. Amber ran away because she was afraid. Mr. Amber told his friends about what had happened, and they tried to convince him that he was wrong. Mr. Amber rejected his friends' advice. He got into a fight with one of his friends.

As a result, they had to take Mr. Amber to the hospital for a broken nose, jaw, and leg. After Mrs. Amber heard the tragic news, she immediately went to see him. He was ashamed that she saw him in that condition. He used flattering words to persuade Mrs. Amber to forgive him. Therefore, she agreed to forgive him provided that he would go with her to counseling bi-monthly for the next six months. They did not miss one session, and were only late for one. They reconciled their differences and started going to church.

The church can help and nourish these families with the appropriate ministry. There should be family ministries designed to help family members cope with day-to-day conflicts. If and when they are given the right support, they can be a great asset to the church in helping others to become believers that Christ is calling for in these times.

Demonic Ambushes

I found a startling line in a book some thirty years ago which said, "The devil is the first peer and president of hell." That quote stuck in my mind and left an indelible mark. The devil, the first peer and president of hell, is a tough statement. It is tough because the devil is in charge of the activities of hell. Those who are not of God are already living in a hell mentality. After thinking about that quote, I immediately thought about Satan's purpose, plan, presence and power. Satan's purpose is to deceive and destroy the mind of the believer so that the believer will submit to Satan's way of life. His plan is to destroy, his presence is to intimidate and his power is to influence.

Satan ambushes and attacks directly. Many people do not

know how to handle these attacks. We are facing a dangerous enemy, an enemy that's constantly on our trails, day and night. Every time Satan comes our way, he comes in the form of disguise. He deceives us. "Satan masks himself as an angel of light. The Ephesians believers were acquainted with Satan's attempts to transform himself into a benevolent power."[60]

As said earlier, Satan's intent is to take full control. Full control can't begin until someone has been captured. In the military, when one is captured, he or she is taken prisoner of war or killed, one or the other. When you are ambushed by Satan you will not be delivered until the Holy Spirit intervenes. When Satan ambushes one, it means to be ambushed in the mind. Those who are ambushed, their minds are trapped with foolishness, pride, jealousy, deceit, fraud, lying, etc.

When Satan captures a person, there is really not a moment of bargaining or to work out a deal. In essence, this is not a hostage situation. In a hostage situation, the one who is in control is looking for something in the place of the hostage. There is some type of ransom involved; but in this case, there is no ransom to pay. When Satan has captured you, your soul is at stake. There is nothing to bargain in place of one's soul. Satan desires all of his hosts to end up in hell. Demons ambushed Adam and Eve; demons ambushed all of Joseph's brothers and turned them into political plotters. They plotted against Joseph from every angle. All of what they were doing was demonic. They were cunning, deceptive, sadistic and egotistical. In essence, they were all for themselves because of hate (Genesis 37:1–8).

Only demons persuade one to attempt to kill. This plan is designed to destroy the plan that God has outlined for the church. Oh what a surprise attack. It is planned for every church and individual. Satan desires to satisfy his kingdom. Satan's presence is to dominate every child of God. Paul said, "When I want to do good, evil is right there with me" (Romans 7:21b). Christians must keep praying in order to break down and destroy the presence of Satan in everyday living. The power of Satan attacks the weakest point of every believer, and if one does not have faith he or she can be intimidated by this power. Satan's power is to try and overtake every believer, especially those who are new to the faith.

Breaking Down Strongholds

This is a real battle. It is a challenge that we have to encounter. We can't allow these strongholds to get the best of us. *Believers must be prepared when they encounter stronghold powers.* They will attack the mind, body, soul and spirit. Rick Renner in his book, *Dressed to Kill,* says this concerning strongholds, "When strongholds are rooted in the mind, they are rooted deeply. Only the Holy Spirit provides a 'strategy' on how to pull them down. He will show you how to use those God-given weapons, and He will show you when and what to attack!" [61] The believer must be open to the leading of God regarding how to deal with these strongholds. Strongholds are not leaving because of whom we are; our position, influence or status will have no bearing.

In Ephesians 6:10, Paul says, "Finally my brethren be strong in the Lord and in the power of his might." The word "finally" comes from the Greek phrase, *tou loipou,* which is translated for the rest, the conclusion of a situation. Paul uses this phrase in the epistle to mean the matter has come to a head. It is really and truthfully over. It can't be changed. In order to break down strongholds, one has to be final in his or her conclusion regarding standing firm on the word of God.

The book of Ephesians is a straightforward book in that its message regarding facing spiritual warfare is encouraging. "Grace and peace to you from God our Father and the Lord Jesus Christ" (Ephesians 1:2). The message is that Christians are covered by the unmerited favor of God. It is mercy that no one deserves, and peace from God is ultimately the good news of the Gospel. We can stand firm on the Word of God because we have His grace. We have grace to keep us while in battle. We must be aware of the movement of the enemy, "Similarly if we underestimate our spiritual enemy, we shall see no need for God's armor, we shall go out to the battle unarmed, with no weapons but our own puny strength, and we shall be quickly and ignominiously defeated."[62] Christians have the power and the weapons to dismantle the strongholds of the enemy. Having these spiritual arsenals and utilizing them is to be seen. Therefore, the harsh and evil tactics of Satan must at no time intimidate Christians.

The church, the Body of Christ, needs to join forces against the enemy twenty four seven. When I was a teenager in church in Georgia, there was an old song that the church used to sing, "Satan we're going to tear your kingdom down." This song was sung with that intention, with much fervor and power. The seasoned saints of the church were serious. The church must mean business. Ready or not, here we come. Even today, believers should take the same stance and don't be abashed when it comes to letting Satan know that the evil kingdom must and will come down.

It is imperative that believers take a serious look at what Paul is saying to the Ephesians, "Put on the full armor of God so that you can take your stand against the devil's schemes" (Ephesians 6:11). This is what is needed in order to take on severe strongholds. We have to be fully dressed in order to do that. When we are fully dressed, it is a sign that we are ready for battle. If we walk around undressed, we are subject to injury from the evil one. Being undressed is also non-decent. Sin will make one feel undressed. That is what happened to Adam and Eve in the Garden, they were naked.

The responsibility of disciples must show respect in the Body of Christ and be examples for others to follow. We can't break down strongholds when we do not take responsibility and walk by faith. Remember, Satan intends to distract and discredit our discipleship. Regardless of what happens, we must keep our resolve, stand firm and use the Word of God to conquer every path we trod, whether on the mountain or in the valley.

STUDY REVIEW GUIDE: THE CHURCH UTILIZING POWER THROUGH CONFLICT

Biblical Truth

Christians must fight sinners and not saints.

Key Word

WARFARE: The Greek word for warfare is *strateia*, which means "an host or an army"

Memory Verse

Ephesians 6:10

Point of Emphasis

Saints fighting saints will only impede the progress of kingdom work. It will also weaken spiritual strategy.

Theological Reflection:

Your theological views and reflection from this study.

Personal Application:

Your thoughts regarding spiritual warfare.

Study Questions

1. Why is it that the church loves to fight the church, and how can the saints help avoid others from fighting in the Body of Christ?

2. How can some innocent believers stay away from traps set by Satan?

3. How much do you think that the church is prepared to fight warfare?

4. How does the biblical truth apply to you?

5. How can strongholds be broken in your life, church and community, and what is the role of the church in this area?

The Church's Most Respected Identity

Having the Power to Stand

> "Now I say to you that you are Peter, and upon this rock I will build my church, and all the powers of hell will not conquer it. And I will give you the keys of the Kingdom of Heaven. Whatever you forbid on earth will be forbidden in heaven, and whatever you permit on earth will be permitted in heaven" (Matthew 16:18–19, NLT).

It is very important that every church takes a bold stand for Jesus.

The witness of the church has lost something over the centuries because many churches have not been standing up because of a weak foundation. They have not been standing up to the principles in God's Word. There is a grave need to rediscover the sacred art of discipleship. The test of the church is contextually in these verses. Here Jesus gave His disciples a lifelong lesson. Jesus did not waste His time developing and training disciples to sit around to do nothing. The church is not in the sitting business, the sleeping business, nor the standing business, in the sense of being idle. God does not need sanctified sitters, but sanctified saints. The church is not to sit on the premises, sleep in the pews, nor stand in the way of the truth. I remember the long time running game show in the sixties: *To Tell the Truth.* The emphasis of the show was to find out who was the true person. There were three individuals and two of them had to pretend that they were the real person. Each was asked different questions and they had to respond. The audience had to determine who the real person was.

When I was young I wondered why they had such a show on television to determine who the right one was. As I reflect over this show, I am reminded about how it relates to the church. There are many individuals in the church, and some are acting like they are disciples when in fact they are not. They walk like disciples, but they are not. They put on a good game, but are far off course. When pertinent questions are asked, they stumble to give the right answer. Sometimes, their patience ran out when they could not answer.

Facing Oppositions

When oppositions come to one, they come to all in the Body of Christ. "Our greatness is unleashed in the context of community. When we move together, God is most perfectly revealed in us."[63] The New Testament church has been and now is challenged by various oppositions in society. Challenges come every day, week, month, year, decade, and so on. The church is challenged to hold up the blood stain banner of the Lord Jesus. She is unlike all other institutions in that she stands alone anchored in faith, saturated in grace, and established in love. The church stands as an umbrella of mercy and justice. Regardless of these oppositions, the church must stand up in these times and take a stand for right and righteousness, truth, mercy and peace. Many times one will have to stand alone. The church must be real in her motive and approach and cannot remain a sleeping giant in a lively world. The church must put faith into action. It does not help to say one thing and do another. The walk must match the talk. There are many buried talents, undiscovered treasures, unconscious insights, and unfulfilled tasks. With these oppositions, the church must move on in a positive manner.

Peter's Confession

Peter was destined to confess Jesus as the Christ. He was appointed by God to do so. When Jesus asked the question, He said to them, "But who do you say that I am?" (Matthew 16:15, NKJV). Jesus was curious about how the question would be answered. He was not concerned about what others were saying, but them. He was checking up on their knowledge regarding discipleship. He wanted to know about their commitment. Peter spoke on behalf of the other disciples. They probably were baffled when Jesus asked the question. They could have felt ashamed because they did not know the answer. His confession was revealed by the Holy Spirit when Peter said, "Thou art the Christ the Son of the Living God."

This was when Christianity was born. Christianity has its total rule and authority in Christ. So therefore, Peter's confession was a confession of Christianity. It was a theological confession. It was theological because it was an expression of faith, conviction and assurance. The authenticity of the confession gave the disciples the encouragement to stand up as the real church. Ever since Peter's confession, the church has been standing and standing tall. His confession left an indelible mark on the church. Simon Peter was no longer the same. He was transfigured by his own answer. When we are asked today who Jesus is, all we have to say is Jesus is the Christ, the Son of the living God. The Son of the living God has a special ring to it. It means something. It says something and it stands for something because the "gates of hell shall not prevail against it" (Matthew 16:18, NKJV). There are dots, bows and arrows that the devil will try to use to destroy and upset the church, but the devil can't conquer.

Peter's confession drove a hole in the devil's strategy which was planned for the church. This happened because "the Old Testament furnishes us with a record of the origin of the church in recounting God's relationship to Israel. The primary factor in this relationship between God and Israel is that God called Israel as His chosen community."[64] As God called Israel as His chosen community, the church is God's chosen community to proclaim His glory. The Master called His disciples together to test them and to find out about their role as real disciples. Real disciples make a big difference for the kingdom of God because real disciples have an allegiance to Christ. It has to be noted that Christ is the center of attraction because of what God has done. If the church wants to be a credible herald, witness, and effective messenger of God, then it must constantly proclaim the message of Jesus to the world. In these last days, a church that forgets what its purpose is will utterly fail, simple as that. No believer wants to see any church fails; however, there must be constant prayer, support and encouragement for those churches that forgets its purpose here on earth.

The Church Under Construction

Jesus said, "And I tell you that you are Peter, and on this rock I will build my church, and the gates of Hades will not overcome it" (Matthew 16:18). The church is still under construction because there are many who have not surrendered to Christ. Some people are trying to play hard to get. They know that they want to accept Jesus, but some are afraid of what others might say. There are other religions that disown them and even threaten them if they accept Christ. The completion of the church will be done when Christ returns. We have to rightfully say that the church is under construction and not reconstruction. While the church is under construction, individuals are being developed spiritually in order to become effective witnesses for Christ. Reconstruction means that the church was built and destroyed. The temple was destroyed but not the Ekklesia. While the church is under construction it goes through seven phases before completion: (1) Praying for direction (2) The phase of finding the right soil to build on (3) Cultivating the ground (4) Pouring the foundation (5) Building the walls (6) Laying the roof and (7) The dedication of the ministry to God. These phases can be used when a church is planting another church.

Praying for direction. This is the most important phase. The purpose for doing anything for God depends on the efficacy of prayer. Prayer puts meaning on purpose. Prayer puts strength on strategy and, last, prayer puts all things in order. It recognizes God as the head of all creation and purpose in life.

The right soil. This phase is an important phase. It is important because the church here finds it purpose, statement of belief and vision. The Bible says, "Where there is no vision the people perish" (Proverbs 29:18, KJV). This phase sets the tone for building a credible ministry.

Cultivating the Ground. Cultivating the ground is the target area that has to be worked. Cultivation in this context means to minister to individuals and prepare them for the receptivity of the gospel. This also involves nurturing and getting to know people in the area. If this phase is not handled with care and love, the outcome of the ministry will suffer. Many churches started without cultivation. It is important to build on a solid foundation. This phase gets the church ready for the next endeavor.

Pouring the foundation. It is now time for the real test. Here the right foundation is on Jesus. The Bible says, "A person must build his or her house on the rock" (Matthew 7:25). House here represents a relationship in Christ. The church can use this same biblical principle to build people happier and healthier lives in Christ. When this phase is complete, the rest of the building program is a testimony of the previous work. When pouring the right foundation, one must dig deep so that the foundation will last forever. I read when they built the Brooklyn Bridge, it took seven years because they could not reach the ground. The bridge had to be tested before it was cleared for completion. Vehicles could not be driven on it until it had a strong foundation. There are many strong foundations in the world. These foundations were not built overnight. It took time. It will take time for the church to build strong lives for Christ. The church has to build right and stay on the right foundation. This means that Jesus builds the church. We are the workers in the field, going after those who need the solid foundation through Christ.

Building the walls. The walls of the church could refer to three things: (1) strength (2) protection and (3) privacy. The church needs to make sure the walls are built strong. This means that the believer's spiritual life must be stationary. One of the most important parts of a building is the walls. The walls protect the privacy of those who are in the building. Each believer is protected by the blood of Jesus. There are many weak walls that do not have stability and structure. Believers need to really have their walls built. The walls are preparation for the roof.

Laying the Roof. Metaphorically, laying the roof is hard. Roof in the context of discipleship is a covering. It is a covering because Jesus is the head. Laying the roof takes skill. If the roof is not laid properly, leaks will occur. And when leaks occur, other damage occurs as well. There are many churches that do not have the right roof. That is why there are always leaks. Leaks here refer to being inadequate in the Body of Christ.

Dedicating the Ministry to God. Dedication does not come until what has been built is completed. Individuals involved in ministry must remember that God blesses efforts for those who remain dedicated to the task at hand. When dedication takes place, it is the evidence of hard work and long hours of preparation. When the ministry has been blessed by God, God validates the ministry and it is recognized by God as authentic.

Using the Keys of the Kingdom

One of the most prominent shortcomings of the church is the failure to use the keys of the kingdom. Disciples must know what the keys are and how to use them. Jesus said, "And I will give you the keys of the Kingdom of Heaven. Whatever you forbid on earth will be forbidden in heaven, and whatever you permit on earth will be permitted in heaven" (Matthew 16:19). Keys are a symbol of authority. When Jesus said "I give you the keys," He was giving authority to Peter. The main key to the kingdom is the gospel of our Lord and Savior Jesus Christ. This key is the foundation for the rest. Peter used the authority that Jesus gave him to open the door of salvation for the Gentiles. The testimony of Peter is one of the keys. Churches must have a testimony regarding their faith. Other keys of the kingdom are prayer, worship, faith, and mercy. The church is not much without authority.

The church was built upon the confession of Peter. The disciple's authority was through Peter. This was an honor bestowed on the disciples, authority to open heaven. The keys show authority of believers, that is to say the church as it relates to discipleship. If God has an indictment on the church, it would be the lack of using the keys to the kingdom.

Therefore, the leadership of the church has the keys. The church needs to use the keys more in order to be effective kingdom builders and workers. The church is using the wrong keys, and it is impossible to do any binding. When you are trying to use keys that do not fit, nothing is going to open or happen, absolutely nothing. Jesus put confidence in Peter and later His disciples to represent Him in regards to binding and losing (Matthew 18:18). This means that the church's authority is in the keys. This is when discipleship is being completely implemented. The church needs encouragement to keep the keys. This means that the church must be identified with having the keys. No keys no kingdom. It is important that the church understand the different keys to be used.

The church has been given the authority to bind and lose. In fact the church has been given the role of God's Spiritual Law Enforcement Agency. Those who disrespect God and the church will be subject to arrest and can only be released by the church. The world is really at the mercy of the church. Now the church cannot function in regard to losing and binding when it is not in the will of God. The church cannot bind and lose when sin and disobedience lies at the door of the church. This brings us to the next component. When Jesus gave the keys to the disciples, it was also about leadership. He also had a broader view for the use and understanding of the keys. The next section explains this view in detail.

Keys for effective leadership serve as a model in the church. There are effective keys to unlocking the future for rediscovering leadership in the church. This is what the kingdom is about. Keys are the basic principles for good leadership and living. Keys help individuals to communicate and interact while utilizing faith. A good leader is one who plans every phase of work through prayer and fasting as the keys of the kingdom are integrated in the life of the believer. I want to suggest what Jesus was talking about when He said, "I give you the keys:"

Faith. The key of faith is crucial in the life of the believer. One cannot do anything without it. Faith is an important key in the life of the believer. One must live a life of prayer and have total faith in God. The Bible says, "And without faith it is impossible to please God, because anyone who comes to him must believe that he exists and that he rewards those who earnestly seek him" (Hebrews 11:6).

Righteousness. This key is the key that really points out our relationship with Jesus. Righteousness is seeking to live in the will of God and walk upright with dignity, class and respect. It is striving to live up to God's standards and seek to please God in every facet of life. A true believer is not happy until he or she is walking in righteousness.

Obedience. Jesus taught His disciples to follow Him and be obedient. One of the greatest weaknesses in the church is probably disobedience. Many are so accustomed to disobedience until they think it is a rightful part of life. This is because it is a programmed trait in the church, home and community. In actuality, people know disobedience is wrong, but continue to be disobedient. I say this because most of us have our own agendas.

Love. People are longing to be loved. This means that believers must show and demonstrate God's **Agape** love. We must also show **Phileo** love, which is brother and sister love. Jesus expected his disciples to make sure this key fit the purpose for their lives. There is no substitute for wisdom. Jesus said, "I am sending you out like sheep among wolves. Therefore be as shrewd as snakes and as innocent as doves" (Matthew 10:16).

Wisdom. Wisdom must be used for God's glory and not our personal gratification. Although wisdom is one of the gifts of the spirit, all believers must have wisdom in order to make intelligent decisions for God. There is no way to be effective as a believer without wisdom. Wisdom is the direction that the church needs to go. Wisdom is connected to understanding. One must be wise enough to understand. The Bible says, "for wisdom is more precious than rubies, and nothing you desire can compare with her" (Proverbs 8:11).

Knowledge. One cannot be a dedicated and loyal disciple without knowledge of God. It is not enough to know about God, but one must have a thirst for knowledge about God, Jesus and the Holy Spirit. The Bible says, "I myself am convinced, my brothers, that you yourselves are full of goodness, complete in knowledge and competent to instruct one another" (Romans 15:14).

Ethical living. All that we do as Christians is no good if bad conduct exists. This is a good example about Christian living. The church represents Jesus. Listen to what Paul said to the Church at Philippi, "Whatever happens, conduct yourselves in a manner worthy of the gospel of Christ. Then, whether I come and see you or only hear about you in my absence, I will know that you stand firm in one spirit, contending as one man for the faith of the gospel" (Philippians 1:27). Too many believers are tricked by the devil to do things that are not becoming of God. We can't live loose lives and expect God to bless us as kingdom builders.

Patience. Disciples must have the key of patience. Jesus

had patience with His disciples. The Bible says, "Here is a trustworthy saying that deserves full acceptance: Christ Jesus came into the world to save sinners—of whom I am the worst. But for that very reason I was shown mercy so that in me, the worst of sinners, Christ Jesus might display his unlimited patience as an example for those who would believe on him and receive eternal life" (1 Timothy 1:15–16). It is imperative that believers have patience with those who are ministered too.

The Purpose of Authority

The church only has authority through Jesus. No Jesus, no authority. The purpose of authority in the church is to fully represent the Godhead with integrity. This means doing the will of God. We do the will of God by seeking what is His will. The church's sole authority is in the authority of Jesus Christ. This means that the church must be ethical in all its dealings and interactions. There must not be any misleading of any sort whatsoever. Authority in Christ gives the church Christological credibility. This means that Christ is the center and focus of the church. It does not mean for the church to use its authority in a wrong manner. The Bible says, "The Pharisees heard that Jesus was gaining and baptizing more disciples than John, although in fact it was not Jesus who baptized, but his disciples" (John 4:1–2). This is using authority in the right manner. It is also being obedient. The church must take a stand regardless of how people understand or view the church and the power in which it is used. However, in reality, people see the church differently.

Regardless of how different people see the church, the purpose and power of authority remains the same. Authority can be used in the context of different ways authority is viewed. Some see the church as a dressing room for saints as a way to catch the next cloud to heaven. Some come to church to enjoy their weekend religious jag, and that's all they want. Some see the church as a political action group. Some see the church as legislating morality. Some see the church as a hospital, healing the sick in a sin sick world. Hans Kung states," If we see the church as the people of God, it is clear that the church can never be merely a particular class or caste, a group of officials or a clique within the fellowship of the faithful."[65]

There are those who view the church as a beacon light, pointing souls to Christ. Regardless of the different views, the real church still has authority because it stands in the midst of everyday life. It makes unusual claims for itself and displays unusual qualities and justification of them. The question is, how do you view the church? How one sees the church is really an image of the church. The image can be positive or negative. Every believer must have a closer walk with Jesus. Believers should have a strong conviction for Christ. They should be willing to stand up for Jesus at any cost, and at any time. If Peter had conviction, we need to today. We can't survive without it. Our purpose for using authority is to ultimately glorify God and represent God. Authority means that believers have been commissioned to carry the gospel to the ends of the earth. God given authority in the life of the church is what drives the church to adequately represent God while facing oppositions, circumstances and even complaints. The real church cannot be lax and remain in comfort zones when God is expecting authoritative kingdom building work.

Those who are representatives of the real church will do

whatever it takes to please God. The real church is the discipling church. "The discipling church is at least three things: a hospital for the spiritually sick, a greenhouse for the growth of new believers, and a training center for the eager and well."[66] The above image of the church is total representation of what the real church should do.

The serious and busy pastor will implement the hospital image, the green house and training center. This is exactly what Jesus commissioned His disciples to do in the Great Commission. The church should be about teaching, training and also troubleshooting. A troubleshooter knows what to do when in any given situation. A troubleshooter studies different scenarios for different problems. There are times when a problem comes in the church and needs some directions. Troubleshooting means that there are guidelines to fix and repair problems and help bring healing to individuals. The real church really must have troubleshooters. One cannot be a troubleshooter when he or she is the trouble. We are either troublemakers or troubleshooters. Troubleshooters will know what to do when spiritual technical problems occur. Jesus' disciples were trained as troubleshooters.

The Early Church, the Church at Ephesus and the Church at Philippi were among those of the real church. All of these churches had a discipleship plan. The Early Church was dedicated to helping each other. "They devoted themselves to the apostles' teaching and to the fellowship, to the breaking of bread and to prayer" *(Acts 2:42)*. Devotion is a sign of a real church. They fellowshipped daily. The word for fellowship is *koinonia,* meaning to worship together, or to have a common relationship under the guidance of the Holy Spirit. It is not drinking coffee, tea, or eating. That is socializing. That comes after real fellowship.

Only true disciples can stand up. Jesus said, "For every tree is known by his own fruit" (Luke 6:44a). The real church must produce fruit. Jesus intended for His disciples to produce fruit. The Bible says, "I am the true vine, and my Father is the gardener. He cuts off every branch in me that bears no fruit, while every branch that does bear fruit he prunes so that it will be even more fruitful" (John 15:1–2). A disciple is known by a certain lifestyle and what he or she produces in the Christian walk and character. Non-disciples cannot produce real fruit. Fruit is love and being productive for the kingdom of God. One cannot fake producing real fruit. It has to be real. Fruit bearing will be shown because of a dedicated lifestyle.

In regard to being the real church, the Ephesians had a mind to work. They were using authority in their ministry. They were committed to living as Christians of light while walking in the truth (Ephesians 4:17–32). Paul reminded them of their relationship with the Lord Jesus. The Church at Philippi was just as serious as the Church at Ephesus. They were encouraged by Paul to be imitators of Christ's Humility (Philippians 2:1–5). The teachings of Christ were meant for others in the Body of Christ in addition to His disciples. Disciples today must be totally committed to the Great Commission. Therefore, the real church is the Body of Christ and not just only a segment of churches. The church must stand with principles, priorities and unity.

STUDY REVIEW GUIDE: THE CHURCH'S MOST RESPECTED IDENTITY

Biblical Truth

The church of God must at any cost stand on the word of God.

Key Word

SEEK: The Greek word for seek in this context is *ekzeteo*, which means "to seek out or after, to search for" The prefix ek means out. So it means out from something.

Memory Verse

Hebrews 11:6

Point of Emphasis

Being able to stand is a prerequisite for the church to be a greater witness for Christ.

Theological Reflection

Your theological views and reflection from this study.

Personal Application

Your thoughts on how this study has impacted you.

Study Questions

1. How has Peter's confession made an impact on the Devil's strategy?

2. Which leaves a greater impact on the church, oppositions in or those out of the church?

3. What evidences can the church show for standing on the Word?

4. How does the biblical truth relate to your ministry?

5. What is the purpose of authority in the church?

The Church's Life-long Purpose

Praying with Power

> "Therefore confess your sins to each other and pray for each other so that you may be healed. The prayer of a righteous man is powerful and effective" (James 5:16).

It is your Christian duty to pray with a Godly purpose.

What is it like for a church to pray with a purpose? God's purpose in our lives is to communicate with Him in everything we do. Genuine prayer is making the right connection with God through the Holy Spirit and power. This communication is through prayer. Many times we get mad with each other and do not speak for days, weeks, months and years. That has no purpose and it really short circuits our spirituality. When the righteous pray, it really moves God to action. When the righteous pray, God becomes available more. When the righteous pray, eyes and ears are more open to its surroundings. There is a closer connection to God when the righteous prays. Believers should have the passion of prayer like the Psalmist. The Bible says, "May my prayer be set before you like incense; may the lifting up of my hands be like the evening sacrifice" (Psalm 141:2). Incense is a Latin term. It means "to burn." The aroma overpowers the very presence of evil. The Psalmist is stressing the importance of praying to the point that prayer becomes an aroma before God. Incense in prayer is a symbolic blessing of the living God. E. M. Bounds, a noted expert on prayer, says, "The prayers of God's saints are the capital stock in heaven by which Christ carries on his great work upon earth."[67]

Many ancient nations used incense in their ceremonies. The purpose of prayer is to walk with God daily. It is not just to wait until a tragedy occurs in our lives, families and communities. We should keep close to the heartbeat of God. At some point all of us, whether Christians or non-Christians have been broken in spirit because of circumstances in our lives. These circumstances have weighed heavily and we all have handled them differently. There are two choices, we are either broken or pray until there is a breakthrough. Bruce Wilkinson wrote, "Our God specializes in working through normal people who believe in a supernormal God who will do His work through them."[68] Prayer is the source of God's connection to His people. When there is a need for a dynamic breakthrough, God is always willing to show up. When was the last time you showed up for an appointment with God? Has God been calling you to the moment of prayer and you stayed in bed, or kept being preoccupied with your own agenda. Only you can answer that question.

The Persistency of Prayer

God's will is for all to pray with persistency and power. The Bible says, "Men ought always to pray, and not to faint" (Luke 18:1, KJV). The Greek word for faint is *enkakeo*, which means to lack courage, lose interest, or give up. People must pray and never give up. This means to pray and believe that God will answer according to His will. God's purpose is connected to our persistency in praying. We must be determined and unrelenting. The problem is that many of us don't stay the course when it comes to praying, except when tragedy comes. The sadistic, blatant and vile tragedy of 9/11 touched millions of Americans and other countries. People from all walks of life turned to God in prayer. As a result of 9/11, many developed a fruitful life of prayer, and others went back to business as usual. God is watching our intentions. God's church is the praying station on earth that represents heaven.

There are other passages in the New Testament regarding the persistency of prayer. In 1 Thessalonians 5:17, Paul is concerned that the church at Thessalonica prays. He says, "Pray without ceasing." The word in the Greek for ceasing is *adialeiptos*. This Greek word means that prayer is constantly recurring, it keeps on happening and is uninterrupted. This word *adialeiptos* is an adjective in Greek, meaning from the negative *dia*, to go through. Therefore, Paul is encouraging the church to get their prayers through.

Furthermore, to the church at Ephesus, Paul says, "And pray in the Spirit on all occasions with all kinds of prayers and requests. With this in mind, be alert and always keep on praying for all the saints" (Ephesians 6:18). Emphasis is on the word keep. The Greek word for keep in this verse is *diatereo*, to carefully keep and to go through. Saints in the Body of Christ must always make prayer a priority. Paul tells the Colossian Church the same. He says, "Continue steadfastly in prayer, being watchful in it with thanksgiving" (Colossians 4:2, ESV). The Greek word for continue is *proskartereo*, which means to continue strong or press your way. Believers must pray earnestly in the Spirit and never giving up on their purpose for praying.

The church can't fail to pray because prayer is a form of worship. If people can't rely on the church for fervent prayer, this is a sign of undernourishment. If this is the case, then the church may need to go in a spiritual incubator and receive round the clock treatment from the Holy Spirit before she can be able to effectively minister to the world. The above metaphor describes what heaven can and will do for individuals who pray persistently, they will keep in contact with God. God is looking for persistent prayer warriors who are permanent, but are not temporary. This means that one must have great tenacity to stay the course. Many times the devil tries to convince believers to throw in the towel. He wants people to give up. If believers give up, then there is no testimony. He is not worried about non-believers, but those who are close to the heartbreak of God. The purpose of persistency is this: If you are sleeping, wake up, get up, pray up and God will make you up. He will give you what you really need for your daily walk.

David's remorse of his unfaithfulness to God brought him

to seriously talk with God regarding his spiritual plight when he had committed adultery with Bathsheba. "Have mercy on me, O God, according to your unfailing love; according to your great compassion blot out my transgressions" (Psalm 51:1). God remembered David and restored his lost joy. The entire 51 Psalm is a prayer that David prayed with an intense heart. God had compassion because his heart was focused on making restitution with God. God honored his request and as a result, he was blessed. Prayer is the link to God that keeps open communication.

Prayer guides us through the toughest storms and battles. Prayer is what carries us from moment to moment. It is the divine link to God's riches in heaven and for our survival on earth. Don't start your day without prayer, because you never know what you will encounter. You could encounter family problems, neighbors, co-workers and those who you accidentally run into. God is waiting for you to respond to the heavenly response. God is eagerly waiting on our prayers.

The Intenseness of Prayer

In II Kings, there is a remarkable account of prayer. Hezekiah prayed to God because of his desire to live after Isaiah the son of Amoz told him that he would not live. He was gravely sick. When he heard the depressing news of his demise, he turned to God. His prayer was not only persistent, but intense. Because of the intenseness of Hezekiah's prayer, God was moved. Hezekiah had no other recourse but to turn to God. He evidently did not play with his request to God. God favors those who earnestly come before him in sincere prayer. Intenseness is the recompense of prayer. In this case Hezekiah was rewarded fifteen more years. Hezekiah reminded God of his past dedicated and committed life.

God's favor was in the life of Hezekiah. It was because He prayed with intenseness and persuasion. His heart and soul were in his prayer. Nothing evidently distracted him from reaching the heartbeat of God. It is the duty of each believer to pray like Hezekiah. His prayer was in the context of life and death. It was an emergency. All he knew was that he was not ready to leave this world. God felt his passion, persistency and priority. Those who dwell in the secret place of God will win the battles of life.

The Power of Prayer

Living a purposeful life requires that one prays with power. The power of prayer is like a magnet, it just pulls us to the presence of God. Prayer is the believer's spiritual vitamins and iron. It is like breathing air, necessary for life. A lack of oxygen and we will die physically. The same holds true in our spiritual life. A lack of prayer, and we die spiritually and become powerless. Power in prayer is the anchor for the believer's soul. Prayers should be power packed with the anointing of the Holy Spirit. Believers should be prayer driven. Total focus should and must be on the power of prayer. This means that the believer can't really make it without prayer. If there is little or no power in prayer, then prayer has no purpose and will not reach the heart of God and will not experience the blessings of the power of prayer. The believer in Christ must have a direct link to God if he or she wants to be heard. Listen to the language of the Psalmist regarding the power of prayer. "Praise be to God, who has not rejected my prayer or withheld his love from me!" (Psalm 66:20). It is to be commended to the Psalmist for giving God total praise and having the confidence in prayer.

Daniel is a prominent prayer warrior in the Old Testament. His prayers were intense, powerful and persistent. There are many others in the Old Testament who prayed with conviction, priority and passion and most of all with a purpose. When I say purpose I mean with a stated request made to God. Solomon prayed for strength. Jacob prayed, Samuel prayed, Elijah prayed, Moses prayed, David prayed and Hanna prayed. Elijah had a purpose for praying and he had a direct link to God. God showed favor in Elijah's life. "The praying of Elijah is a demonstration of the supernatural power of prayer. His prayers were miracles of power."[69] God was able to trust Elijah because of his strong prayer life. Elijah was a strong figure in the Old Testament. He was the John the Baptist of the Old Testament. God favored his humble prayer life. He was really determined. God was with him in everything he did. Elijah had the command of God in his life. He was a man of faith and faith was a vital part of his life and testimony.

Prayer of Thanksgiving

Praying with a purpose requires that every prayer has the segment of thanksgiving. In fact, every prayer should be packed with thanksgiving. The Bible says, "Do not be anxious about anything, but in everything, by prayer and petition, with thanksgiving, present your requests to God" (Philippians 4:6). Prayer of thanksgiving is essential for every element of praying. Every request made known to God will be answered because of thanksgiving. The Greek word for Thanksgiving in Philippians is *eucharistia*. In the New Testament this word and other companion words are widely used. The prefix *eu* in *eucharistia* means "well." It means to do well or to feel good about something. *Charistia* comes from the Greek word *Charis*, which means grace. When the word *Charis* is compound with *eucharistia*, which is a noun, it means to have good favor.

In I Timothy 2:1, Paul sincerely prays for all persons. He uses *eucharistia* to bestow good favor or wonderful blessings for the church. He says, "Urge, then, first of all, that requests, prayers, intercession and thanksgiving be made for everyone." This prayer of thanksgiving is a prayer related to worship. Paul was saying that in order to worship, everyone must pray for each other. When the church uses this verse, God will bestow heavenly favor upon the church. There are many other references where *eucharistia* is used. It is important that the church seriously pray for each other. Have you seriously thought about praying for someone today, or right now? Take the time now and ask God to bless someone.

God is waiting to bless the believer with heavenly blessing. That is why Paul says, "And my God will meet all your needs according to his glorious riches in Christ Jesus" (Philippians 4:19). It is guaranteed that if and when one prays and trust God, God will honor and show favor in the believer's life. Thanksgiving is a spiritual benefit that God gives because He loves us. When we give God thanks, heaven is glorified. Thanksgiving in prayer is a form of praise. When we praise God we bow and honor Him in the Holy Spirit. Praying in the spirit of thanksgiving really pleases God, and the believer's soul will be blessed forever. When the believer thanks God in prayer, it authenticates the prayer and validates a spiritual union with God that is a lasting connection.

The believer must have the faith and confidence to trust God completely. Thanksgiving is to thank God for allowing you to be able to approach Him in the moment of prayer. In every prayer, heavy emphasis should be on thanksgiving. At the time of prayer, one should thank God for being able to pray. It is thanking God in advance for answering your prayer. It is another way of asking God for grace. God highly deserves our thanksgiving because of His faithfulness in our lives.

Jesus and Prayer

Elijah may have been chosen as a great example of prayer in the New Testament, but regardless of all the prayer warriors in the Bible, none could match the prayer life of Jesus. Jesus had a purpose on this earth, and He had a purpose for praying. One of the strongest and intense prayers of Jesus was in the Garden of Gethsemane. "Then Jesus went with his disciples to a place called Gethsemane, and he said to them, "Sit here while I go over there and pray." He took Peter and the two sons of Zebedee along with him, and he began to be sorrowful and troubled. Then he said to them, "My soul is overwhelmed with sorrow to the point of death. Stay here and keep watch with me" (Matthew 26:36–38).

Jesus was on a mission, and he had a special time and place to pray the above prayer. He was sorrowful because of sin on His shoulders for the world. He was burdened with the agony of sin because he was getting ready to be arrested and be crucified. This prayer meant something to God. It was intense, powerful and passionate. Jesus was ready for Calvary before he went to the Garden. He had been with God long before the last night in the Garden of Gethsemane. This powerful prayer was an example for his disciples. They did not have enough faith to stay wake one hour. You can't pray and sleep. They do not mix. God is looking for our undivided attention. Jesus laid the ground work for praying with a purpose. He had a purpose for praying for His disciples. He said, "My prayer is not for them alone. I pray also for those who will believe in me through their message, that all of them may be one, Father, just as you are in me and I am in you. May they also be in us so that the world may believe that you have sent me. I have given them the glory that you gave me, that they may be one as we are one" (John 17:20–22). Just as Jesus prayed for His disciples, pastors and church leaders must pray for one another. In this prayer, Jesus is really asking God for marching orders for His believers. Marching orders keeps believers in cadence with the Holy Spirit. We cannot get out of step with the Holy Spirit. The Holy Spirit is our guide.

Our Lord Jesus emphasized the Our Father's Prayer. He knew it was substance, spirit and power in that prayer. Jesus' prayer was a model prayer. "One day Jesus was praying in a certain place. When he finished, one of his disciples said to him, "Lord, teach us to pray, just as John taught his disciples" (Luke 11:1). In this passage, Jesus was committed to praying and praying in the Spirit. It was not unusual for Jesus to find a place of solitude and spend time with the father. The disciples wanted to really learn how to pray. That is why they asked him that question, "Lord teach us to pray"...."Jesus teaches not merely what and how we are to pray, but He teaches prayer. He is the revelation of prayer."[70] Jesus is qualified to teach people to pray because of his divine status with the Father. He is our intercessor. Since Jesus intercedes for us, we need to intercede for others.

While on this earth, Jesus thoughts were prayerful thoughts embedded in the Holy Spirit. Every word He uttered was a word connected to prayer. He was God's mystery on earth. People of status could not figure him out. The Bible says, "The Son is the radiance of God's glory and the exact representation of his being, sustaining all things by his powerful word" (Hebrews 1:3). God is Holy in nature and the Son is Holy in nature. His prayers were Holy prayers. They were accepted by God because prayer is His business. His life was marked with prayer. He completely represented God for He was about doing the work of His Father. Jesus refused to do anything without praying. His aim was to teach His disciples how to pray. When Jesus teaches one to pray, he or she is a certified prayer warrior for the kingdom of God. After having been certified, there is nothing that will hinder or stop a true believer for being a true kingdom builder.

At the very beginning of His public ministry, Jesus prayed and prayed with intense power. As a result of his prayers, God moved in His life and gave Him spiritual support and strength. Now is the time to set priorities and give God the best in spiritual intimacy through the power of prayer.
After having read this book on discipleship, God is expecting you to pray with a purpose and stay the course. It is your responsibility to encourage someone else to become a dedicated disciple and understand the message of *The Sacred Art*. As Paul encouraged Timothy in the ministry, he says "I thank

God, whom I serve, as my forefathers did, with a clear conscience, as night and day I constantly remember you in my prayers" (2 Timothy 1:3).

STUDY REVIEW GUIDE: THE CHURCH'S LIFE-LONG PURPOSE

Biblical Truth

Christians must be in the business of praying.

Key Word

CEASING: The Greek word for ceasing is *adialeiptos*, which means to constantly recur.

Memory Verse

Luke 18:1

Point of Emphasis

If one fails to pray and pray consistently, one will live a life of temptation.

Theological Reflection

Your theological views and reflection from this study.

Personal Application

Your thoughts on how this study has impacted you.

Study Questions

1. Why is there a lack of pouring out to the Lord in prayer in churches and individual lives?

2. Do you think many in churches have a set time to pray, or do they pray when trouble comes?

3. How much do you think that the church is prepared to fight warfare?

4. How does the biblical truth apply to you?

5. What should one do when one has been deeply hurt, should they cool off first and pray later or pray for strength? Discuss the difference.

Embracing Social Justice with Power

The Church's Radical Identity

> "For The Son of Man did not come to destroy men's lives but to save them" (Luke 9:56).

The church must lead in the fight for social justice. In order to be a true disciple of Christ, one must be concerned about social justice. A working definition for social justice is the concept that every individual or group would be treated equal. The church is being watched. There are merging trends built around social justice issues. Can the church be true to the gospel of Christ and be silent on social justice issues? The church must be radical about embracing the total person. Jesus approached issues with passion and power. Many have viewed radicalism as a negative response to injustice. In order to fully understand social justice issues, it is necessary to take a look at social analysis. Social analysis deals with people as well as issues. "Social analysis can be defined as the effort to obtain a more complete picture of a social situation by exploring its historical and structural relationships."[71]

I am not in anyway a proponent of the social gospel movement. The social gospel movement is liberal Christian thought. Its primary purpose is to look at the gospel message and embrace how one lives and is treated. However, I do believe that there is a need to embrace social issues and problems. It can in no way replace the gospel message and it is no substitute for the fundamental truth. The church can't overlook the ministry of social justice.

It is imperative to look at a social situation in order to see the big picture of the overall situation of both individuals and groups. Social situations deal with social problems and the church must be prepared to respond to such problems. What the system and what systems have done is to show the necessity of how both historical and structural relationships impact our society. What has happened in the 30's and 40's is not exactly the same as today. However, the impact regarding emotional stress as a result of historical and structural relationships still remains the same today. People are hurting.

The Social World of the Hebrew Prophets

The social world of the Hebrew Prophets is a world of distinction among the prophets. The Hebrew canon of scripture carries a collection of books called the prophets, both Minor and Major prophets. There are twelve minor prophets and four major prophets. The Prophets sets the tone for the rest of the Bible regarding social issues and problems. The prophets sound the alarm regarding bridging social justice issues. All of the prophets were in their own culture and world. "Although the world of the prophets and their audiences often revolved around urban centers like Jerusalem, Bethel and Samaria, it was agriculturally based. During the period from 1000 to 587 b.c.e., most of the population still lived in small farming communities of 100–250 people."[72] I will refer to three Hebrew prophets who embraced social injustice in their day, Micah, Amos and Hosea, who are Minor Prophets. All of the prophets had to contend with the aristocrats of their day. Some were more verbal than others. Micah was one whose ministry was a ministry to those who were disenfranchised. He says, "He has showed you, O man, what is good. And what does the LORD require of you? To act justly and to love mercy and to walk humbly with your God" (Micah 6:8). Micah was referring to a holistic ministry during that time. His intent was to speak to address the issues of his day. He was saying to really take action to love mercy and walk humbly before God. If and when this is done, justice will be addressed.

The ministry of Amos was a ministry of social justice. He saw the need to address the issues of his day. He was concerned about the poor. The people of his day were overlooking and mistreating the poor. The wealthy were not concerned about the welfare of the poor and less fortunate. Amos says, "I hate, I despise your religious feasts; I cannot stand your assemblies. Away with the noise of your songs! I will not listen to the music of your harps. But let justice roll on like a river, righteousness like a never-failing stream!" (Amos 5: 21, 23, 24) Amos was really a role model for the rest of the prophets regarding speaking and preaching against injustice.

While the prophets were concerned about social justice, they were concerned about the people. They all had a different calling, but basically emphasized the same problems among the people.

Their conception of the Word of God was aligned with their belief of Yahweh. Their message was the message of Yahweh. The message of Hosea was not exactly the same of his contemporaries. The major difference was that Hosea had to save a nation and redeemed them by the assignment that God gave him regarding marrying a prostitute. Israel had left God and was in danger of God's Punishment. Their chance of return was through Hosea. They had committed injustice against God by sinning. The Bible says, "Hear the word of the LORD, you Israelites, because the LORD has a charge to bring against you who live in the land: "There is no faithfulness, no love, no acknowledgment of God in the land" (Hosea 4:1). God's case against Israel was that they had broken the divine laws of justice. They did not treat God right. Hosea had to bring them back to God first before he could deal with social issues with them.

The prophets had to proclaim the divine message regardless of the intensification of problematic issues of their day. "Their concern was not the faith, not even the 'message': it was to deliver a specific message from Yahweh to particular men and women who, without themselves being aware of it, stood in a special situation before God."[73] Amos, Hosea and Micah focused their attention to specific social justice issues to bring closure to the plight of the human situation of their day.

Part 3: The Power Factor

The Social World of Jesus

Jesus' ministry was a ministry of mingling with people. He was born in a Jewish culture. His culture was part of the economic standards of His day. The social world of Jesus was influenced by what people thought and how they interacted with each other. One question of importance is how did first century people think about themselves and what they really thought about Jesus? Jesus surely knew how and what people thought about Him. How did Jesus handle social issues of His day? He was busy accessing the social situation of individuals and families. I am sure questions came up like, did the people of His day think He was charismatic? His aim was to identify with people in order to effectively minister to their needs. His culture dictated that he had a life, and that life was in the social environment of Judaism.

Jesus' social world included the area of Palestine, Galilee and Jerusalem. His mission was to the Jewish people. "Social world refers to the socially constructed reality of a people, that nonmaterial "canopy" of shared convictions which every human community erects and within which it lives, and which is sometimes known simply as "culture."[74] Let us look at issues during Jesus' Day. He dealt with the issue of the poor, depraved, outcast, and burdened. He interacted with people from every class of His world. Jesus was concerned and he made provision for people. The Bible says, "Jesus called his disciples to him and said, "I have compassion for these people; they have already been with me three days and have nothing to eat. I do not want to send them away hungry, or they may collapse on the way" (Matthew 15:32). He wanted to make sure that the social justice issues were dealt with in a timely manner.

Was Jesus concerned about social justice issues? This question set the tone of this chapter. It sets the tone because it probes the very fiber of our thinking and the context of ministry. The social world of Jesus was concerned about current issues and concerns. He did not come to destroy, but to save. Jesus was in touch with the people and their plights. He knew their pain, rejection and isolation for the community. The very reason that Jesus was rejected was because of his stance and standards regarding the Kingdom of God. He was considered an outcast as well as a threat. In fact, he did not fit in the flow of the community. His agenda was not in touch with those of status.

The Social World of the Church

The church is in the center of the community. People pass by hourly, daily, weekly, monthly and annually. In one sense they are checking out the church in regards to the response of those who are crying for nurture, care and attention. In the context of the ministry of the church, social justice is the cry to aid the poor, weak, disenfranchised and outcast. The church lives among people who are in need of assistance. Their needs need to be met and looked over. The church needs to do social discipleship, meeting people where they are. Paul commends the Thessalonians regarding their love for each other. "We ought always to thank God for you, brothers, and rightly so, because your faith is growing more and more, and the love every one of you has for each other is increasing" (2 Thessalonians 1:3). Charity is the link to helping people from all walks of life.

People are waiting on charity. The church can't avoid people because they will get the attention of the church one way or another. The community and individuals look to the church for direction, regardless of the size of the church.

There are those in the church with issues as well as those outside. Both need care and love. The church cannot just shout at every worship service, sit and remain a sleeping giant when it comes to speaking out against social justice issues. Sermons and teaching workshops should address social issues. We know that Dr. Martin Luther King, Jr. was the advocate of the social justice movement through the Civil Rights Movement. He was not only concerned about the welfare of African Americans, but all people.

The church has to minister in the midst of issues such as affirmative action. Churches have to deal with racial and sexual discrimination. Members of all congregations are in one way affected by social issues as well as others. "The response to social crises that comes from the Christian community will depend largely upon the triangular relationship between the word, the preacher, and the congregation."[75] Regardless of the cultural context of the congregation, every church should have ministries focused on at least one of the following social issues such as: human rights, unemployment, education, HIV AIDS, drug abuse or alcohol.

The Social World of the Family

The family is an integral part of society. This means that the family is a major part of culture and everyday interactions. The family has to deal with social problems that can and will affect the lifestyle of individuals. It can be positive or negative. There are so many families who need housing, clothing, medical care, employment, education and food. Using the issue of hunger, Jesus worked a miracle in the presence of a large crowd. The Bible says, "Jesus called his disciples to him and said, "I have compassion for these people; they have already been with me three days and have nothing to eat. I do not want to send them away hungry, or they may collapse on the way" (Matthew 15:32). If you would read the rest of the chapter you will find that He fed four thousand and five thousand on another occasion, in Luke's account he fed five thousand (see Luke 9: 14).

It does not stop with the above issues. Other major issues are: child abuse, spousal abuse, elderly abuse, and educational neglect. All of these issues are part of family violence. The church can be an asset to the family and support them in getting help regarding their issues. If the church is not an asset, then it can be a liability in the sense of remaining silent. Therefore, churches should integrate in their discipleship ministry, workshops on the above issues. Although many of these issues are personal, at some point they become public.

Educational neglect and truancy are sweeping the country. Children are not being sent to school and many are truant. Churches can and should encourage families to make sure that children go to school. An attendance incentive program at the church recognizing students who have perfect attendance may encourage those who have poor attendance to improve. Helping families deal with their issues is the radical response of the church. The community and the church should work together and network and bridge the gap regarding the issues of social justice and social problems. When the church becomes sensitive to these issues, the ministry of discipleship becomes practical, touching people where they are and identifying with their plight. Therefore, families and individuals need the support of the church through the teaching of the Word of God and prayer. Individuals need the assurance from church leaders and believers that Jesus is the answer to their problems while they are trained to become faithful and growing disciples in God's Church.

STUDY REVIEW GUIDE: EMBRACING SOCIAL JUSTICE WITH POWER

Biblical Truth

The church must care about the total person.

Key Word

COMPASSION: The Greek word for compassion is *eleeo*, which means "to show kindness."

Memory Verse

Mark 5:19

Point of Emphasis

Social justice is one major focus of the gospel message.

Theological Reflection

Your theological views and reflection from this study.

Personal Application

Your thoughts on how this study has impacted you.

Study Questions

1. Is social justice part of the Gospel message? If not, why not?

2. Do you think many in churches are seriously embracing social justice issues?

3. How does social justice affect the church and the family?

4. How does the biblical truth apply to you?

5. Should social justice issues be mentioned from the pulpit, if not why?

Appendix 1

The Disciple's Pledge

God, after reading this book, *The Sacred Art: Growing Faithful Disciples in the Twenty-First Century,* I am inspired to be a better disciple. In order to fully understand my purpose as a disciple, I pledge full allegiance to God, Jesus and the Holy Spirit as a true disciple of Jesus Christ. I will honor God at all times as a servant in his church daily by being obedient to God's will in my life.

I pledge to pray daily spending time with God, studying His Word, "showing myself approved" and walking by faith. I will honor God by being a faithful steward. I pledge to make an attempt to witness and lead others to Christ in fulfilling the Great Commission.

As a disciple, I pledge to defend the Christian faith from any negative predators who try to discredit God, Christ, the Holy Spirit and the Body of Christ. I also pledge to forgive others because Christ has forgiven me for my sins. It is my honor to live a life that is well pleasing in your sight.

1. I will honor God by advocating respect for the Body of Christ as well as others in the local and global community.

2. I will strive to develop a stronger relationship with God and other disciples in order to fully represent Christ.

3. I will strive to encourage new believers as well as seasoned saints to stand up against the antics of the devil.

4. I will support my local church family financially to help advance the kingdom of God.

Appendix 2

A Theology of Discipleship

The ministry of discipleship is a ministry that cannot be overlooked. It cannot be overlooked because every ministry in the church is related to discipleship. Our declaration is that our faith is built on Jesus Christ. Jesus is our Lord and Savior. The fundamental task of discipleship is to have total allegiance to God. The joy of discipleship is being obedient to the gospel of Jesus Christ. It is sharing with others the meaning of being true disciples. Following Jesus today is to compare master-disciple relationships as it was in Jesus' day. Today as it was in ancient Judaism, we are following in the footsteps of Jesus. The pattern Jesus set for the Jews and His disciples is also meant for the modern church today. Jesus intended for His disciples then and now to live a sanctified life. There must be a relationship between our salvation and discipleship, between discipleship and ministry.

There are many leaders in churches today confused as to what one should do as disciples. There should not be any confusion. The confusion comes when there is a lack of clarity and direction for believers to follow. I have tried to explain what a disciple is and what a disciple does. Disciples are not disciples for themselves, but a disciple for the kingdom of God. Their purpose is to be an example for others and help lead them and nurture them into authentic disciples of Christ.

Discipleship is a life–long endeavor. The Bible says, "Then Jesus said to his disciples, "If anyone would come after me, he must deny himself and take up his cross and follow me" (Matthew 16:24). Jesus was telling His disciples that they have to follow Him because it is a life-long endeavor. One cannot follow Jesus with his or her own agenda. One must be willing to give life and follow Jesus.

It has been well said that one who is a disciple is a follower and learner of Christ. One cannot be a disciple without having a relationship with Christ. Discipleship is similar to that of a doctor and a surgeon. One becomes a doctor before becoming a surgeon. This means that one must be trained to become a doctor first and then become a surgeon. The same holds true for a disciple and a specialized servant. One becomes a disciple before entering a specialized ministry. The emphasis is being a true and faithful disciple of Christ.

Epilogue

It is my hope that this book will make a great difference in your life. I pray that something I have said will encourage you to rethink, refocus and redefine what it means to be a faithful disciple. I have argued that it is our responsibility to be dedicated and real disciples of Christ. Being real disciples authenticates our relationship with Christ. If discipleship is not significant, then there is no valid relationship.

There is no church, pastor, or lay person that can substitute any other work for the work of being faithful and dedicated disciples. Each believer has a God *"calling responsibility"* to fully represent Christ in a contaminated and sinful world. Jesus says, "But I, when I am lifted up from the earth, will draw all men to myself" (John 12:32). To lift Jesus up is to walk in His ways and to live out his purpose; this is the focus of discipleship.

The time is long overdue for churches and believers to identify with the "Jesus Movement." It is my conviction that the Jesus movement is the movement of God that is required to move the heart of God. Many churches have been living in the shadows of discipleship. Discipleship is the total lifestyle of each believer, and church. Churches have to do corporate discipleship as well as individual discipleship. This is evident in the Great Commission (Matthew 28:18–20). The Great Commission is the biblical account of discipleship.

Pastors, preachers, and evangelists must emphasize and take the leadership regarding the focus of discipleship in the local church. If discipleship is missing in churches, then the other aspects of ministry will suffer, such as stewardship, evangelism, mission and Christian education. The church has to reclaim the emphasis of discipleship. Discipleship must be relevant, practical and persuasive. Jesus has his eyes on the church to deliver the message of the ministry of discipleship.

There are a lot of resources today for churches to take advantage of regarding building faithful disciples. Therefore, the church needs to return to the sacred art of growing faithful disciples. It is obvious that many churches will see the need to make new and fresh strides toward a celebrative ministry of discipleship. A celebrative ministry of discipleship means that individuals and churches are excited about identifying with Christ in bringing new life and a brighter future for believers experiencing the love of God.

The Apostle Paul thanked the church at Thessalonica regarding their faithfulness as disciples. He said, "We always thank God for all of you, mentioning you in our prayers. We continually remember before our God and Father your work produced by faith, your labor prompted by love, and your endurance inspired by hope in our Lord Jesus Christ" (1 Thess: 1: 2–3). The Thessalonians was another church emphasizing discipleship character other than the early church in Acts, the Church at Ephesus and the Church at Philippi.

We are living in a time when the church must reach out

EPILOGUE

under the guidance of the Holy Spirit. Believers must accept total responsibility to be genuine followers of Christ in a difficult world. Pastors must lead. The church must refocus the ministry of discipleship encouraging the church to step up to the plate and get on first base and make a home run for nurturing new and mature disciples for the glory of God. I encourage all churches to join in and support the message of the Great Commission regardless of one's culture or faith tradition.

As I have passionately labored to write and share these words with you, it is my prayer and hope that the ministry of discipleship will have an indelible and lasting effect on individuals and churches to take a stand for building faithful disciples for the benefit of the Kingdom of God. I encourage all believers to look at the biblical, theological and spiritual context of discipleship and move forward with love, faith, commitment and accountability for growing healthy disciples in such times as these.

ENDNOTES

Introduction: Why The Church Should Care About Making Disciples?

1. Howard Thurman, *The Centering Moment* (Richmond, VA.: Friends United Press, 1980), p. 65.

Chapter 1: A Theology of Discipleship

2. George Barna, *Growing True Disciples: New Strategies for Producing Genuine Followers of Christ* (Colorado Springs, CO.: Water Brook Press, 2001), p. 115.

Chapter 2: Understanding the Biblical Plan of Discipleship for God's Church

3. Win Arn, and Charles Arn, *The Master's Plan for Making Disciples* (Grand Rapids, MI.: Baker Books, 1998), p.24.

4. Bill Hull, *The Disciple-Making Church* (Grand Rapids, MI.: Fleming H. Revell), 1990, p. 43.

5. Henry T. Blackaby, and Claude V. King, *Experiencing God: Knowing and doing The Will of God* (Nashville, TN.: Lifeway Press, 1990), p.109.

6. Walter A. Henrichsen, *Disciples are Made not Born* (Wheaton, IL.: Victor Books, 1988), p. 64.

7. Robert E. Coleman, *The Master Plan of Evangelism* (Grand Rapids, MI.: Fleming H. Revell, 1993), p. 27.
8. Marcus Borg, *Jesus A New Vision* (New York: Harper & Row Publishers, 1987), p. 59.
9. William Barclay, *The Letter to the Philippians, Colossians and Thessalonians* (Philadelphia, PA.: The Westminster Press, 1975), p. 38.

Chapter 3: Tending to the Missionary Assignment

10. Carl Fielding Stewart, *African American Church Growth, Twelve Principles for Prophetic Ministry* (Nashville, TN:. Abingdon Press, 1994), p. 118.
11. Win Arn, and Charles Arn, *The Master's Plan for Making Disciples* (Grand Rapids, MI.: Baker Books, 1998), p.54.
12. Paul A. Beals, *A People for His Name: A Church-Based Missions Strategy* (Grand Rapids MI.: Baker Book House, 1988), p. 13.
13. Ibid., p. 16.
14. Dwight J. Pentecost, *Design for Discipleship: Discovering God's Blueprint for the Christian Life* (Grand Rapids, MI.: Kregel Publications, 1996), p. 9.
15. Dale Galloway, *The Small Group Book: The Practical Guide for Nurturing Christians and Building Churches* (Grand Rapids, MI.: Fleming H. Revell, 1995), p. 43.
16. Joel Comiskey, *Home Cell Group Explosion:How Your Small Group Can Grow and Multiply* (Houston, Tx.: Touch Publications,1998), p. 17.

Chapter 4: Working a Ripe Harvest

17. Rick Joyner, *The Harvest* (New Kensington, PA.: Whitaker House, 1997), p. 21

ENDNOTES & BIBLIOGRAPHY

18. Johnny Turner, *Rebuilding the Walls: A Call to Teaching in The African-American Church* (Brooklyn, NY.: Word for Word), 1998, p. 5.
19. Jerry M. StubbleField, *Ministering to Adults* (Nashville, TN.: Broadman Press, 1986), p. 185.
20. Rick Warren, *The Purpose Driven Church* (Grand Rapids, MI.: Zondervan Publishing House, 1995), p. 49.
21. Lee Strobel, *Inside The Mind of Unchurched Harry and Mary* (Grand Rapids, MI.: Zondervan Publishing House, 1995), p. 83.
22. See St. John 4:1–13
23. St. Luke 19:1–6
24. Mark 5:24–29
25. Mark 5:30–34
26. George G. Hunter, III., *Church for the Unchurched* (Nashville, TN.: Abingdon Press, 1996), p. 31.
27. Bill Bright, and James O. Davis, *Beyond All Limits: The Synergistic Church for a Planet in Crisis* (Orlando, Fl.: New Life Publications, 2002), p. 47.
28. Mark 5:35–36
29. Mark 5: 37–43
30. John 11:1–6
31. John 11:7–13
32. John 11:14–20
33. John 11:21–27
34. Ken U. Fong, *Pursuing the Pearl: A Comprehensive Resource for Multi-Asian Ministry* (Valley Forge, PA.: Judson Press, 1999), p. 75.
35. John 11:28–37
36. John 11:38–44

Chapter 5: Growing a Healthy Church

37. Dietrich Bonhoffer, *The Cost of Discipleship* (New York: Macmillan Publishing Co., Inc., 1963), p. 40.
38. Rick Warren, *The Purpose Driven Church* (Grand Rapids MI.: Zondervan Publishing House, 1995), p. 48.
39. Jerry M. Stubblefield, A *Church Ministering to Adults: Resources for Effective Adult Christian Education* (Nashville, TN.: Broadman Press, 1986), p. 179.
40. Walter A. Henrichsen, *Disciples are Made Not Born* (Wheaton, IL.: Victor Books, 1996), p. 127.
41. Dale Galloway, *The Small Group Small Group Book: The Practical Guide for Nurturing Christians and Building Churches* (Grand Rapids, MI.: Fleming H. Revell, 1995), p. 54.
42. Bill Hull, *High Commitment in a Low Commitment World* (Grand Rapids MI.: Fleming H. Reve11,1995), p. 132.
43. Tommy Tenney, *Experiencing His Presence: Devotions for God Catchers* (Nashville, TN.: Thomas Nelson Publishers, 2001), p. 32.
44. E. M. Bounds, *The Complete Works of E. M. Bounds on Prayer* (Grand Rapids MI.: Baker Books), p. 238.
45. Bill Hybels, *Too Busy Not To Pray: Slowing down to be with God* (Downers Grove IL.: InterVarsity Press,1988), p. 75.
46. Harold A. Carter, *The Prayer Tradition of Black People* (Baltimore, MD.: Gateway Press, , 1982), p. 120.
47. Luke 4:14–21

Chapter 6: Philippi: Being a Faithful and Loving Church

48. J. A. Motyer, John, *The Message of Philippians* (Downers Grove IL.: InterVarsity Press, 1991), p. 17.
49. William Barclay, *The Letters to the Philippians, Colossians,*

and Thessalonians (Philadelphia PA.: Westminster Press), 1975, p. 8.
50. Mark Denver, *Nine Marks of a Healthy Church* (Wheaton IL.: Crossway Books, 2000), p. 242.
51. Philippians 2:12
52. Philippians 4:2–3
53. Malcolm Warford, *Becoming a New Church* (Cleveland OH.: United Church Press, 2000), p. 53.

Chapter 7: Engaging in Spiritual Warfare

54. Robert E. Coleman, *The Master Plan of Discipleship* (Grand Rapids, MI.: Fleming H. Revell, , 1998), p. 98.
55. Rick Renner, *Dressed to Kill: A Biblical Approach to Spiritual Warfare* (Tulsa, Ok.:Albury Publishing, 1991), p. 132.
56. Justo Gonzalez, *The Story of Christianity* (San Francisco, CA.: Harper, 1981), p. 7.
57. Acts 5:14–16
58. Richard Ing, *Spiritual Warfare* (New Kensington, P.A.: Whitaker House, 1996), p. 20.
59. Mark 5:1–4
60. Greg Ogden, *Discipleship Essentials, A Guide to Building Your Life In Christ* (Downers Grove IL.: InterVarsity Press,1998), p. 202.
61. Rick Renner, Rick, *Dressed to Kill: A Biblical Approach to Spiritual Warfare and Armor* (Tulsa OK.: Albury Publishing, 1991), p. 37.
62. John R. W. Stott, *The Message of Ephesians* (Liecester, England, Downers Grove, IL.: Inter-Varsity Press, U.S.A., 1975), p. 263.

Chapter 8: When the Real Church Stands Up

63. Erwin Raphael McManus, *The Barbarian Way* (Nashville, TN.: Nelson Books, A Division of Thomas Nelson Publishers, 2005), p. 134.
64. Alvin J. Lindgren, *Foundations for Purposeful Church Administration* (Nashville, TN:Abingdon Press, 1965), p. 39.
65. Hans Kung, *The Church* (Garden City, NY.: Image Books, A Division of Doubleday & Company, Inc., 1976), p. 167.
66. Bill Hull, *The Disciple-Making Church* (Grand Rapids, MI.: Fleming H, Revell. A Division of Baker Book House Company, 1990), p. 41.

Chapter 9: Praying with Power

67. E. M. Bounds, *The Complete Works of E. M. Bounds on Prayer* (Grand Rapids, MI.: Baker Books,1990), p. 299.
68. Bruce Wilkinson, *The Prayer of Jabez: Breaking Through to the Blessed life* (Sisters OR.: Multnomah Publishers, 2000), p. 41.
69. Samuel Chadwick, *The Path of Prayer* (Fort Washington, Pa.: CLC Publications, 2000), p. 86.
70. Adolf Saphir, *Our Lord's Pattern of Prayer* (Grand Rapids, Mi.: Kregal Publications, 1984), pp. 12–13.

Chapter 10: Embracing Social Justice

71. Joe Holland and S. J. Henriot, *Social Analysys: Linking Faith and Justice* (Washington D.C.: Daves Comminucations and Orbis Books, 1984), p. 14.
72. Matthews H. Furnish, *The Social World of the Hebrew*

Prophets (Peabody, MA.: Hendrickson Publishers, 2001), p. 1.
73. Gerhard Von Rad, *The Message of the Prophets* (New York, Hagerston, San Francisco, and London: Harper and Row, 1967), p. 100.
74. Marcus J. Borg, *Jesus a New Vision: Spirit, Culture, and the life of Discipleship* (New York: Harper and Row, 1987), p. 79.
75. Kelly Miller Smith, *Social Crisis Preaching: The Lyman Beecher Lectures* 1983 (Macon, GA.: 1983, Mercer University Press, 1984), p. 28.

Bibliography

Barclay, William. *The Letters to the Philippians, Colossians, and Thessalonians,* Philadelphia, Pa.: Westminster Press, 1975.

Barna, George. *Growing True Disciples: New Strategies for Producing Genuine Followers of Christ.* Colorado Springs, Co.: Water Brook Pres, 2001.

Beals, Paul A., *A People for His Name: A Church-Based Missions Strategy.* Grand Rapids MI.: Baker Book House, 1988.

Birch, Bruce C, & Rasmussen, Larry L., *Bible & Ethics in The Christian Life,* Minneapolis: Augsburg, 1989.

Blackaby, Henry T, and King, Claude V. Experiencing God*: Knowing and Doing The Will of God.* Nashville, Tenn.: Lifeway Press, 1990.

Bonhoffer, Dietrich. *The Cost of Discipleship.* New York.: Macmillan Publishing Co., Inc., 1963.

Borg, Marcus J. *Jesus a New Vision: Spirit, Culture, and the Life of Discipleship.* New York.: Harper & Row, 1987.

Bounds, E. M., *The Complete Works of E. M. Bounds on Prayer.* Grand Rapids, Mich.: Baker Books, 1999.

Brandow, Doug. *Beyond Good Intentions: A Biblical View of*

Politics. Wheaton, Ill.: Crossway Books: A Division of Good News Publishers, 1988.

Bright, Bill, & Davis, James O., *Beyond All Limits: The Synergistic Church for a Planet in Crisis.* Orlando, FL.: New Life Publications, 2002.

Carter, Harold A. *The Prayer Tradition of Black People.* Baltimore.: Gateway Press, 1982.

Chadwick, Samuel. *The Path of Prayer.* Fort Washington, Pa.: CLC Publications, 2000.

Coleman, Robert E. *The Master Plan of Evangelism.* Grand Rapids, MI.: Fleming H. Reveıı,1993.

Coleman, Robert E. The Master Plan of Discipleship. Grand Rapids, MI.: Fleming H. Revell,1998.

Comiskey, Joel. *Home Cell Group Explosion: How Your Small Group Can Grow and Multiply.* Houston, Texas: Touch Publications, 1988.

Denver, Mark. *Nine Marks of a Healthy Church.* Wheaton Il.: Crossway Books, 2000.

Eims, Leroy, *The Lost Art of Disciple Making.* Grand Rapids, MI.: Zondervan Publishing House, 1978.

Fong, Ken, U., *Pursuing the Pearl: A Comprehensive Resourse for Multi-Asian Ministry.* Valley Forge, Pa.: Judson Press, 1999.

Galloway, Dale. *The Small Group Book: The Practical Guide for Nurturing Christians and Building Churches.* Grand Rapids, MI.: Fleming H. Revell, 1995.

Gonzalez, Justo. *The Story of Christianity.* San Francisco: Harper & Row,1981.

Hans, Kung. The Church. Garden City, N. Y.: Image Books, a Division of Doubleday and Company, 1976.

Holland, Joe, Henriot, S.J. *Social Analysys Linking Faith and Justice.* Washington, D.C.: Daves Communications and Orbis Books, 1984.

Hull, Bill. *The Disciple-Making Church.* Grand Rapids, Mich.: Fleming H. Revell. A Division of Baker Book House Company, 1990.

Hull, Bill. *High Commitment in a Low Commitment World.* Grand Rapids, MI.: Fleming H. Revell, 1995.

Hunter, George, G. III., *Church for the Unchurched.* Nashville, Tenn.: Abingdon Press, 1996.

Hybels, Bill. *Too Busy Not to Pray: Slowing Down to be With God.* Downers Grove Ill.: InterVarsity Press, 1988.

Ing, Richard. *Spiritual Warfare.* New Kensington, Pa.: Whitaker House, 1996.

Joyner, Rick. *The Harvest.* New Kensington, Pa.: Whitaker House, 1997.

Lindgren, Alvin J., *Foundations for Purposeful Church Administration.* Nashville, Tn.: Abingdon, Press, 1965.

Masters, Phillip Le. *Discipleship for All Believers.* Scottdale, PA. and Waterloo, Ont.: Herald Press, 1992.

McManus, Erwin Raphael. *The Barbarin Way.* Nashville Tn.: Nelson Books, A Division of Thomas Nelson Publishers, 2005.

Motyer, J. A., John. *The Message of the Philippians.* Downers Grove, IL.: InterVarsity Press, 1991.

Ogden, Greg. *Discipleship Essentials: A Guide to Building Your Life In Christ.* Downers Grove, IL.: InterVarsity Press, 2004.

Oliver, Edmund, H., *The Social Achievement of the Church.* Vancover, BC.: Regents College Publishing, 1998.

Pentecost, Dwight, J., *Design for Discipleship:Discovering God's Blueprint for the Christian Life.* Grand Rapids, MI.: Fleming H. Revell, 1996.

Renner, Rick, *Dressed to Kill: A Biblical Approach to Spiritual Warfare.* Tulsa, Ok.: Albury Publishing, 1991.

Sapher, Adolph, *Our Lord's Pattern of Prayer.* Grand Rapids, MI.: Kregel Publications, 1984.

Smith, Kelly Miller, *Social Crisis Preaching. The Lyman Beecher Lectures.* Macon GA.: Mercer University Press, 1984.

Stewart, Carl Fielding, *African American Church Growth. Twelve Principles for Prophetic Ministry,,* Nashville, TN.: Abingdon Press, 1994.

Stott, John R. W., *The Message of Ephesians.* Liecester, England, Downers Grove, Il.:Intervarsity Press, 1979.

Strobel, Lee, *Inside the Mind of Unchurched Harry & Mary.* Grand Rapids, MI.; Zondervan Publishing House, 1995.

StubbleField, Jerry, M., Ministering to Adults.: *Resources for Effective Adult Christian Education.* Nashville, TN.: Broadman Press, 1986.

Tenney, Tommy, *Experiencing His Presence. Devotions for God Catchers.* Nashville, TN.: Thomas Nelson Publishers, 2001.

Turner, Johnny, *Rebuilding the Walls: A Call to Teaching in the African American Church.* Brooklyn: Word for Word, 1998.

Von Rad, Gerhard, *The Message of the Prophets.* New York.: Harper & Row, 1965.

Warford, Malcolm, *Becoming a New Church.* Cleveland, Oh.: United Church Press, 2000.

Warren, Rick, *The Purpose Driven Church.* Grand Rapids, MI.: Zondervan Publishing, 1995.

Wilkinson, Bruce, *The Prayer of Jabez: Breaking Through to the Blessed Life. Sisters,* OR.: Multnomah Publishers, 2000.

Yetman, Norman, *Life Under the "Peculiar Institution: Selections from the Slave Narrative Collection. Ne*w York.:Holt, Rinehart and Winston, Inc., 1070.